A Hunger for God:
Ten Approaches to Prayer

Edited by William A. Barry, S.J.
and Kerry A. Maloney

Sheed & Ward

Chapters 8 and 10 of this book were first published in *Review for Religious* whose editor graciously granted permission to reprint in this volume.

Sheed & Ward™ is a service of National Catholic Reporter Publishing Company, Inc.

Library of Congress Catalog Card Number: 91-61107

ISBN: 1-55612-452-X

Published by: Sheed & Ward
                 115 E. Armour Blvd. P.O. Box 419492
                 Kansas City, MO 64141-6492

To order, call: (800) 333-7373

Contents

For Jim, Corey, Erin, Andrew, and Jacob
  in whom the Mystery has drawn near, again.

For the Jesuit Community at Boston College
  who helped make this book possible.

Introduction

At 6:30 p.m. on September 19, 1988, the editors nervously wondered how many people would show up for the beginning of a new series of talks on prayer sponsored by the Jesuit Community and the University Chaplaincy at Boston College. We had entitled the series "The University at Prayer" and had scheduled twelve sessions, six in each semester. The invitation read:

> In our hunger for God prayer is our very bread. Without it we cannot know or sustain our relationship with the Divine. In twelve sessions we will explore some of the rich variety of approaches to prayer and spirituality in the Christian tradition as we listen to presentations and pray together. Come, "break bread" with us.

We had asked various members of the Boston College community to make the presentations and had reserved the Conference Room of the Jesuit residence, St. Mary's Hall, which could hold up to forty people. On the outside chance that more might come we had reserved the chapel at St. Mary's Hall which could hold up to two hundred people. We need not have been anxious. It quickly became evident that we would need to use the chapel as faculty, administrators, undergraduate and graduate students, and neighbors and alumns of the University began to pour in. In the question period after the talk and prayer session one faculty member got up and said, "I expected about ten people, and look how many of us are interested in prayer." We were, of course, surprised and very pleased. And the interest continued with some fluctuations in numbers for the next two years.

Each talk was followed by a time to pray in the way suggested by the presentation. The quality of the quiet time was part of the atmosphere of "breaking bread" together which we had hoped to achieve. Moreover, because the participants continued to represent the whole community connected with Boston College, we, in fact, did become, in microcosm, the University at prayer. The interest has continued into the third year of the series which, because it is the Ignatian Year, is concerned with themes of the *Spiritual Exercises*.

Boston College is a Catholic and Jesuit university. Hence, God has to be at the heart of what the university is about. As Catholic, the concern with God has to be in a broad sense sacramental. The Catholic tradition takes very seriously the Incarnation and sees the whole world as a sacramental sign of God's presence. According to this tradition there is no hard and fast line between the sacred and the secular. "The world is charged with the grandeur of God," as the Jesuit poet Gerard Manley Hopkins put it. Within the Catholic tradition the spirituality of Ignatius of Loyola, the founder of the Society of Jesus, has its own distinctive characteristics, and these, too, contribute to the ethos of Boston College. Because Ignatius believed in the sacramentality of the universe, believed that "the world is charged with the grandeur of God," he tried to find God in all things and urged his followers to become contemplatives in action. Human beings are not and cannot be always aware of God, but they can, Ignatius believed, become more and more attuned to God's presence with the help of God's grace and by paying attention to their ordinary experience for the signs of that presence. A few examples may clarify what we mean.

The biochemist studying the biochemistry of the brain of a mouse can also become aware of the mysterious Other whose creative love not only makes the mouse but also the biochemist and whose own Spirit arouses the biochemist's curiosity and wonder. The student of Mozart's music can also become aware of the God who loves such beauty. The secretary-receptionist who greets a stranger with a smile can also be aware of the presence of a God who rejoices that two strangers can know that they are brother and sister. Thus the university, or indeed any organization, could always be at prayer if more and more people became conscious of the religious dimension of their lives. We hoped that the prayer series might help people in the university community become more aware of the Mystery at the heart of all our endeavors.

Because these presentations were so effective, we thought that they might be helpful to a wider audience. We had taped the talks and had also asked the presenters to give us a written version of their talk. As we looked over the twenty-four presentations, we realized that some would not survive the translation to print.

Technical problems kept us from using others. In the end we settled for the ten presentations which make up the ten chapters of this book. We are grateful to all those who made presentations during the first two years of "The University at Prayer." We are grateful to Robert Heyer of Sheed & Ward who agreed that the series was interesting and insightful and should be made available to a larger audience. We invite the readers of this book to "break bread" with us.

Part I

Prayer in General

In this first chapter the Benedictine Sebastian Moore, a member of both the theology department and the University Chaplaincy, broaches the question: what does it mean to pray? In his own inimitable style he draws us into the heart of what prayer is about.

1

The Universe at Prayer: What Does It Mean to Pray?

Sebastian Moore, O.S.B.

What I want to suggest in this essay is that prayer is the oneness of mind and heart in the presence of infinite mystery; and that since the split between mind and heart is the essential sickness of our culture, prayer is the most radical therapy for our culture. To learn how to pray is to pass from being part of the problem to being part of the solution—to use a slogan from the much-maligned sixties. Last year at one of our meditation sessions on campus, someone asked "Is there any difference between Transcendental Meditation (TM) and prayer?" It is a question that is always being asked, and it is a very good question. One member of the group answered it in this way: "I took up TM years ago as a therapeutic exercise. Then I found that my meditation was accompanied with a certain longing. I go with the longing."

This experience, which is also my own, enables me to give some definition to the union of mind and heart in the presence of mystery, of which I just spoke. For in disciplined silence, the desire for meaning, which is the thrust of all our living, can begin to be felt in its total trajectory, from the comprehensible goals with which we start to the point where the comprehensible breaks down and there is only feeling to guide us. St. John of the Cross describes this breakdown of meaning with the birth of contemplative prayer:

long-standing methods don't work any more, and there is nothing but this unaccountable longing. Abbot Chapman, with his total honesty, calls it "an idiotic state." This is not a *lapse* from making sense but the breakdown of our attempts to make sense in the presence of truth itself.

Now the birth of contemplative prayer is a growth-crisis to be situated not just in what gets called our prayer-life, but in the whole gamut of human development. For we are born into an overwhelming and unfathomable mystery, that solicits us until we die into its meaning. That solicitation is desire, the Infinite drawing us into its strange perspectives from our small, very finite beginnings. And this means that desire *changes* as we are drawn deeper. In the earliest stages, we think we know what we want; indeed we can be so fascinated by definable and attainable goals that we are hardly aware that it is desire that is giving us meaning. With the central growth crisis experienced as the birth of contemplative prayer, the situation is inverted. The clear, definability factor dissolves, and the desire factor is now all we have to go on, as St. John of the Cross says "with no other light than that which in my heart was burning."

Let me schematize this, for it is really the heart of what I want to say. In the early part of life, desire hides in the known, the clear, the attainable. In the later part, the known is dissolved in desire. Desire, first disguised in its alluring objectives, later sheds this disguise and becomes its naked self yearning for what is incomprehensible. And what this shows is the organic unity between desiring and knowing, between heart and mind. That unity appears first in the knowing, with desire its hidden force. It appears last in the desiring, with the knowing happily serving it in the form of the quiet, repeated, unmeaning mantra or prayer formula.

I hope it is now clearer that in contemplative prayer mind and heart are exercised in their primordial unity. Not surprisingly, we understand the Holy Spirit as, indifferently, the love of God poured out in our hearts, and wisdom. The oneness of truth and love in God touches their oneness at the roots of our being. "Deep calls to deep," as the psalmist says.

It follows from this that contemplative prayer is a touchstone, a focus, in which we may see the university at prayer, the *studium* as *oratio*. A university in the Catholic tradition, which is simply a university that remembers what universities were originally for, namely "to contemplate and pass on what has been seen" (the Dominican axiom), is grounded in the unity of mind and heart which is really the same thing as the unity between reason and faith. It cannot accept the Kantian assertion that the mind is confined to phenomena, while the real, the noumenal, remains beyond its reach, by which I mean unable to fulfill it. I add this last qualification, because in prayer, too, the object is beyond the mind's reach, but not in such a way as not to fulfill the mind. The difference between the Kantian agnosticism and that of *The Cloud of Unknowing* is radical, as I shall have occasion to repeat. In contemplative prayer the mind is at home in that which wholly transcends its grasp; at home there because the heart of the mind is desire, and desire, as I have argued, is the solicitation of the infinite.

Prayer, religious experience, is the denial of the split between mind and heart. What makes William James' *Varieties of Religious Experience* so problematic is that it implicitly accepts this split. James opts for "feeling" *as opposed to* intellect. Not surprisingly, in working within this assumption, he cut himself off from understanding the greatest masters and mistresses of religious feeling. The very thing he was after eluded him. For the truly incomprehensible, in whose presence feeling alone is the response, is what is encountered when intellect at full stretch finds itself powerless and childlike. If I don't believe in intelligence as animated by desire, then I cannot understand the surrender of intelligence when desire is more directly drawn by the mystery which is its meaning. When the author of *The Cloud of Unknowing* says that God is touched "only by love, by thought never," he is saying that mind, as desire, stretches *beyond* thought, not that love is a mindless elevation toward "the divine." Hegel refers contemptuously to the "shrivelling" of religion to "simple feeling, into a contentless elevation of spirit into the eternal."[1] The great teachers of religious feeling were people like Eckhart and Catherine of Siena, who knew desire as the very heart of mind becoming itself in the presence of infinite mystery. And these people tended to be enthusiastic Scholastics. Certainly Eckhart was. One of the recognized effects of contemplative prayer is suddenly seeing the meaning of some particular doctrine. A contempt for doctrine, for saying what can be said, is not a mark of the mystical tradition. Abbot Chapman speaks of contemplative prayer as featuring occasional "flashes of the infinite" in which words like "reality," "eternity," suddenly take fire, interrupting the fog of being "idiotically" passive to "nothing in particular (which is God of course)."[2] More poetically, but less usefully as description, light breaks through the cloud. Mind and heart are one, so that the heart advancing into the unknown can cause resonances in the mind. Perhaps this is what Charles Peguy meant when he said that everything starts as mysticism and ends as politics. And I would regard as suspect any mystical experience today that did not cause some awakening to the hideous plight of most of the inhabitants of the world at this time. Dorothy Day was a great contemplative.

That very descriptive phrase "nothing in particular (which is God of course)" caused leading English Jesuits of the time to seek the condemnation of Abbot Chapman's book in Rome. What I find fascinating about the phrase is that it is at once superbly accurate as description and contains the crucial hint as to how we can recover for the modern world the meaning of God. God, we believe, creates the universe out of nothing. What can this possibly mean? Nothing, I suggest, apart from some reference to contemplative prayer. We know something of the "nothing" out of which God creates: it is the nothing in which the mind, at a certain stage and at important life-crises, loses itself, drawn by desire. Nicholas Lash, in a recent lecture, spoke of "the mystery on the other side of nothing." Is not the first step of Alcoholics Anonymous a stepping into this mystery: the acceptance of my life as totally unmanageable and the surrender to a power not my own? Contemplative prayer, in its many forms and derivatives, *inhabits* creation out of nothing, moves in the rhythm of that all-grounding mystery. The reason why the question of God is so mis-premised today that it is scarcely askable, is that it has been, since the seventeenth century, conceived not in terms of our self-understanding but in terms of what our understanding has discovered, the universe of modern science: God as the ultimate explanation of how it all came together. If God does not explode in the mind when we contemplate the universe, God is not. Two gnomic utterances help me here.

Einstein: "The most incomprehensible thing about the universe is that it is comprehensible." That is the light of wonder at itself going on in the mind. Lonergan: "God is not the explanation of anything. God is the explanation of explanation." Again, the light going on and going out again, leaving us with nothing, with "no other light than that with which my heart was burning." The point is completely missed if we think of God as some super-scientific idea. Where do ideas live?

In the mind. That's where God appears—or not at all. Stephen Hawking, perhaps the greatest modern physicist, speaks in his new book of the possibility of reaching a point where "no new law, or God" would be required to explain the whole.[3] That's pre-Einsteinian. For Einstein, Jewish mystic that he was, it is precisely the comprehensibility of the whole that blows the mind and brings it to the darkness where the heart burns. And it is not surprising that Lonergan latterly was more and more drawn to the mystical, and spoke of it in an increasingly positive way. That is the classic direction for an authentic intellectual to take. As I keep saying, the intellect, being impelled forward by desire, is headed toward the cloud of unknowing in which desire alone can continue its work.

This plunge of the mind into darkness at the moment of insight is illustrated in the classic "proof" that God is, with which Herbert McCabe starts his fine recent book *God Matters.*[4] Why is there anything at all? This question includes all questions. It concerns questioning itself. Why is there why? Why is there the why of things? It asks itself persistently, so it is valid. But a valid question has an answer. So this question has an answer. But since questioning itself is in question, the answer cannot be controlled, defined by the question, as is normally the case with questioning. The answer, then, is incomprehensible, as is "the explanation of explanation." Thus at the moment of realizing that the question "Why is there anything?" has an answer, the mind is plunged into an abyss of mystery. Gabriel Marcel must have been onto this when he said that he had become convinced that there is no difference in kind between the philosopher's and the mystic's way to God. So much for Pascal's "God of Abraham, God of Isaac, God of Jacob, not of the philosophers and savants!" as conventionally understood by a culture that denies God by denying intelligence as the spark of God that becomes fire in the mystic. Interestingly in this connection, Herbert McCabe, in the book just cited, asserts that, despite the conventional idea of the Greeks as questioners and the Hebrews as worshippers, it was the Jews who posed the all-inclusive question about reality itself, which sets them in an unending pilgrimage.

I have tried poetry here:

I ask "Why is there anything?"
And know I have to ask,
And hence know that this questioning
Is an appropriate task.

Therefore there is an answer to
The question I have posed:
Then I reflect: My question too
Seeks to be diagnosed.

The questioning within the whole,
How can the answer be
Within the questioning's control?
Of this it must be free.

A question will direct my grasp
Toward the answer sought.
Asking of all, the sought will clasp
The questioner: I'm caught

In an abyss of mystery
Beyond all reckoning.
Nothing of it is known to me
Save "It grounds everything."

And all desire obeys this law,
Not just desire to know:
Desiring always to be more,
The more takes us in tow.

Why anything? O anything!
The question and the prayer
Alike throw us into the ring,
Its centre everywhere.

The plunge of the mind into darkness at the moment of insight mirrors an existential plunge that is catastrophic: of the disciples of

Jesus from the state of ecstasy induced in them by the contagion of Jesus into the horror of Golgotha whence they are reborn into eternal life by the sight of Jesus risen, the unavowed feeling that this might be a dream brought to awareness and denied by the discovery that his tomb is empty. On this existential contemplative moment that ends the reign of death Christian faith rests, its source the Holy Spirit who draws us into the relationship between the Father and the Son. The prodigious labor of love that is Calvary and Easter dethrones the God we put over us to avoid the mystery, and reveals God as the mystery into whose life we are drawn as into a dance. This horizontalizing of our relationship with God makes sacramental our horizontal dimension, divinizing community as church.

So prayer is desire in its essence as response to the mystery in which we exist. I have argued that in contemplative prayer we have an obscure sense of where the desire whereby we live is headed. I would like to end by looking briefly at another invasion of the mind by desire in its essence, that recorded by C.S. Lewis in a way that, to my knowledge, has no parallel in literature. It comes in his autobiography, *Surprised by Joy*, and in the following, taken from the preface to *The Pilgrim's Regress*.

> The experience is one of intense longing. It is distinguished from other longings by two things. In the first place, though the sense of want is acute and even painful, yet the mere wanting is felt to be somehow a delight. Other desires are felt as pleasures only if satisfaction is expected in the near future: hunger is pleasant only while we know (or believe) that we are soon going to eat. But this desire, even when there is no hope of possible satisfaction, continues to be prized, and even to be preferred to anything else in the world, by those who have once felt it. This hunger is better than any other fullness; this poverty better than all other wealth. And thus it comes about, that if the desire is long absent, it may itself be desired, and that new desiring becomes a new instance of the original desire, though the subject may not at once recognize the fact and thus cries out for his lost youth of soul at the very moment in which he is being rejuvenated. This sounds complicated, but it is

simple when we live it. "Oh to feel as I did then!" we cry; not noticing that even while we say the words the very feeling whose loss we lament is rising again in all its old bitter-sweetness. For this sweet Desire cuts across our ordinary distinctions between wanting and having. To have it is, by definition, a want: to want it, we find, is to have it . . . Lust can be gratified. Another personality can become to us "our America, our New-foundland." A happy marriage can be achieved. But what has any of the three, or any mixture of the three, to do with that unnameable something, desire for which pierces us like a rapier at the smell of a bonfire, the sound of wild ducks flying overhead, the title of *The Well at the World's End,* the opening lines of *Kubla Khan,* the morning cobwebs in late summer, or the noise of falling waves?"[5]

I think that Lewis's "sweet desire" is really, if you'll pardon the banality, "neat desire," desire "in the pure state," the desire which we all live by, as it were isolating itself and stabbing us with its essence.

Let me end by repeating the principle on which these remarks are based. We are born into an overwhelming and unfathomable mystery that will solicit us until we die into it. This solicitation is the meaning of desire. Prayer is creating space for desire to come alive in us and take the mind into that darkness where the first light arises.

Why is there why, the very heart of mind?
The question asks itself, so it is valid.
It has its answer, which we shall not find
Though all the powers that are in us rallied.

The answer, presupposed in very question,
Cannot come to the forefront of our thought,
It stays behind, and is for prayer to rest on,
Incomprehensible, the heart's resort.

Let no one rob us of this inward bliss,
Cloud of unknowing where the heart is drenched,
By telling us of whom it is the kiss:
Thus is the soul out of its climate wrenched.

"Why?" is the life of mind. "Why why?" embarks
On the dark lonely sea where the seal barks.

Part II

Ignatian Prayer

As we noted in the introduction, Boston College is a Jesuit University. It was fitting, therefore, that some of the presentations about our university at prayer should consider Ignatian prayer. Harvey Egan, S.J. of the theology department at Boston College, introduces us to Ignatian prayer. Because of his own cultural predispositions Ignatius uses language that can be upsetting to a modern reader, especially to a modern woman. Mary Garvin, S.N.J.M., who at the time of her presentation was studying at Andover-Newton School of Theology and living in the Boston College community, looks at the *Spiritual Exercises* with a critical, yet sympathetic eye. Finally, William Barry, the rector of the Jesuit Community at Boston College, describes one type of Ignatian prayer, imaginative contemplation of the Scriptures.

2

A Jesuit Looks at Jesuit Prayer

Harvey D. Egan, S.J.

A few years ago, I attended a talk on Zen meditation given by Fr. William Johnston, the well-known Jesuit at Tokyo's Sophia University. He told us to sit in the lotus position, or if we couldn't do that, simply to sit in a chair with our backs straight, and then to concentrate on our breathing, by counting our inhalations and exhalations until we reached ten, and then to begin again. If distracted at any point, we were told to start over. So there we sat in silence for about a half hour until Fr. Johnston said, "That is Zen meditation," and walked off.

Unfortunately, my task here is not as easy because of what St. Ignatius says right at the beginning of his *Spiritual Exercises:*

> By the term "spiritual exercises" is meant every method of examination of conscience, of meditation, of contemplation, of vocal and mental prayer, and of other spiritual activities that will be mentioned later. For just as taking a walk, journeying on foot, and running are bodily exercises, so we call spiritual exercises every way of preparing and disposing the soul to rid itself of all inordinate attachments, and, after their removal, of seeking and finding the will of God in the disposition of our life for the salvation of our soul. (n. 1)

If Jesuit prayer can be identified in some way with Ignatius' *Spiritual Exercises*, then so-called "Jesuit prayer" *cannot* be identified with any one method of prayer. Many writers on prayer incorrectly identify Jesuit prayer with a plodding, step-by-step, recipe method of prayer in which I remember some Christian mystery and reason about it in order to move my will to make practical resolutions that will change my life.

Note well, however, that Jesuit prayer, for Ignatius, has a twofold goal: uprooting our sinfulness, our sinful tendencies, and our disordered loves so that we can seek and find God's will. In fact, Ignatius ended many of his letters with a formula that conveys his pragmatic attitude toward prayer: "May it please the Divine Wisdom to grant that we may always know his most holy will and find our peace and happiness in ever fulfilling it."

In other words, there is a deeply ascetical dimension to Jesuit prayer. With God's help, we have to do everything in our power to get rid of the sin and disorder in our lives. But this ascetical dimension has both a mystical and an apostolic orientation. Jesuit prayer, as far as Ignatius is concerned, should aim at eliminating everything in our being that prevents us from listening to God who conveys his will and from carrying out this will.

Ignatius says this explicitly in the *Spiritual Exercises*:

> But while one is engaged in the Spiritual Exercises, it is more suitable and much better that the Creator and Lord in person communicate himself to the devout soul in quest of the divine will, that he inflame it with his love and praise, and dispose it for the way it could better serve God in the future. (n. 15)

Ignatius was convinced that God deals directly with the person and the person directly with God.

In one of the most extraordinary mystical documents in the entire Christian tradition, two small notebooks, Ignatius' Spiritual Diary, covering the period from February 2 - March 12, 1544 and March 13, 1544 - February 27, 1545, one finds remarks about trinitarian visions and illuminations, various kinds of inner words, profound mystical consolations, mystical touches, and deep mystical joys. However, during this period Ignatius was working on the

Jesuit constitutions and deliberating about a minor point on Jesuit poverty.

What Ignatius wanted during this period was not mystical experience of the Trinity for its own sake. During this whole period Ignatius begged the Father, the Son, the Holy Spirit, Jesus, Mary, the saints, and the whole heavenly court that God's will with respect to this minor point on Jesuit poverty be disclosed so that Ignatius would know with certainty that he was doing God's will.

St. Bernard of Clairvaux or St. John of the Cross emphasized mystical bridal sleep, that is, swooning lovingly in God's loving embrace at the center of the soul, as the most valuable way of serving God, the church, and one's neighbor because in mystical bridal sleep one was doing that for which one was created, namely loving. Ignatius, on the contrary, "uses" his mystical experiences of God to uncover God's will. He did not seek mystical experience, or resting in God, for its own sake, but only insofar as it helped him to seek, find, and execute God's will. Ignatius' mystical prayer has a service orientation. Prayer, for Ignatius, must reveal God's will and then incarnate itself by carrying out that will.

It is one of the ironies of history that the first attacks on Ignatius' *Spiritual Exercises* accused Ignatian prayer of being too mystical, too subjective, too passive, of placing too much emphasis on God's role in prayer, and of actually expecting God to communicate his will to the one making the Exercises. However, later on in Jesuit history, accusations were made that the Exercises fostered too ascetical a prayer, prayer that overemphasized human effort and techniques.

But as we said earlier, precisely because Ignatius expected God to communicate himself and his will to the person, he taught those making the *Spiritual Exercises* to do everything in their power to get rid of anything that could interfere with the divine communication. In short, Ignatian prayer presupposes the mutual interpenetration of asceticism and mysticism, human effort and God's intimate self-communication to the person.

It is instructive to note that many who made the *Spiritual Exercises* under St. Ignatius and the early Jesuits entered contemplative orders, that is, those orders whose members devoted themselves to long hours of prayer. One of the first crises among the early Jesuits was precipitated by some Jesuits who wanted to spend long hours at prayer. Ignatius regarded this as a threat to the apostolic, service orientation of the Society of Jesus. Long hours of prayer meant less time for preaching, teaching, studying, working with the poor and the sick, and the like. And because formal prayer demands so much concentration and energy, long hours of prayer also means less energy for apostolic service.

When some of his men complained that distracting work prevented them from praying deeply, Ignatius insisted that they work with a right intention and direct all that they do to God's honor and glory. He wrote:

> For distractions undertaken for God's greater service and in conformity to his divine will interpreted by obedience not only can equal the union and recollection of deep contemplation, but may even be more acceptable as proceeding from a stronger and more fervent charity.[1]

In short, although Ignatius expected his men to be united with God, he did not consider formal prayer and contemplation as the only way to be so united.

For example, when one recalcitrant Jesuit insisted that eight hours of prayer daily was not enough for him and that a prayer less than two hours long was "no prayer" at all, Ignatius called that bad spirituality and said: "A truly mortified man unites with God more easily in 15 minutes than an unmortified man does in two hours."[2] When someone praised a very holy Jesuit as a man of prayer, Ignatius corrected him and said: "He is a mortified man."[3]

Ignatius was not a man given to exaggeration. Thus, when this saint says that "of a hundred men given to long hours of prayer, the majority of them ordinarily come to grave consequences,"[4] his remarks should be taken seriously. He was referring to pride and obstinacy, and that is why he emphasized mortification and the abnegation of one's will as the key elements for union with God.

In a letter to Francis Borgia, Ignatius suggested that he cut his prayer time in half and that he learn to rejoice in our Lord in a variety of duties and places, instead of only one.[5] In his letter to those in studies, Ignatius writes:

> Keeping in mind the goal of study, because of which the Jesuits in studies cannot spend a long time in prayer . . . they can exercise themselves in seeking the presence of our Lord in all things, in their conversation, walks, in all they see, taste, hear, learn, and in all they do. For it is true that the Divine Majesty is in all things by his presence, his power, and his essence. This method of meditating, that is, finding our Lord God in all things, is easier than that which raises us to the more abstract truths which are made present to us only with much labor. This is a good exercise to dispose ourselves for great visits from our Lord even in a short prayer. Beyond this, they can try to offer frequently to our Lord their studies and labor, seeing that it is for his love that we undertake them, disregarding our own tastes in order that we may serve our Lord in some way and be of help to those for whose life he died. We might well examine ourselves on these two practices.[6]

On another occasion he expressed his mind in this way:

> The fourth way of helping your neighbor is very far-reaching indeed, and consists in holy desires and prayers. The demands of your life of study do not permit you to devote much time to prayer, yet you can make up for this by desires, since the time you devote to your various exercises is a continuous prayer, seeing that you are engaged in them only for God's service.[7]

Instead of concluding his *Spiritual Exercises* with a contemplation of heavenly life (as meditation books in Ignatius's day often did), Ignatius presents the Contemplation to Obtain Divine Love. In this contemplation, one asks for the grace to be a contemplative in action, to be able to find God in all things, as Ignatius was and did. In this exercise Ignatius would have us ask for an intimate knowledge of the many blessings we have received from creation and redemption, to perceive how God dwells in all things, how God works for us in all things, how God dwells in us—that filled with gratitude for all, we may in all things love and serve the Divine Majesty.

In short, for Ignatius, being a contemplative in action is as easy and as difficult as giving ourselves as completely to our daily lives as possible. *Age quod agis,* that is, do what you are doing. Are you supposed to eat, then eat; drink, then drink; sleep, then sleep; work, then work; study, then study; socialize, then socialize; patiently endure suffering, then suffer.

St. Thérèse of Lisieux's "My Vocation Is Love," offers an especially cogent example of Ignatian contemplation in action. Thérèse felt herself called to all vocations: warrior, priest, apostle, missionary, crusader, martyr, and the like. But through contemplative prayer, she was taught that love embraces all vocations and that her vocation was to love. Her "Little Way" consists in filling every moment—no matter how seemingly banal—with self-emptying love. By her unrelenting embrace of the cross and resurrection of daily life, Thérèse was a genuine Carmelite contemplative in action.[8]

Two contemporary examples of Ignatian contemplation in action will summarize my previous remarks. William Callahan, S.J. speaks of a noisy contemplation which is

> to be like Jesus, to be a person who moves in the midst
> of modern noise and tensions both inside and around
> us, and who remains aware of others in loving, bonding
> and caring ways, a person fully present and committed
> with attentive love to all aspects of contemporary life.[9]

Callahan would urge us to pray the day, to pray the news in order to become more conscious of where we can promote faith, peace, and justice.

Inspired by Ignatius' mysticism of finding God in all things, Karl Rahner, S.J., contends that all genuine faith, hope, and love contain at least an anonymous experience of the triune God. Within this context, he speaks eloquently of a mysticism of daily life. Paradoxically, this mysticism appears normally in the grayness and banality of everyday life, in contrast to the often psychologically dramatic way the mysticism of the great saints is manifested.

For example, one may become dissatisfed with one's life, see clearly that things simply do not add up, and yet nurture a real Christian hope in an ultimate reconciliation, agreeing with Julian of Norwich that "all will be well." One may be profoundly lonely, try to love God, to pray, but no answer comes. The heart is left empty, devoid of all emotion and meaning. Perhaps for the first time one has not confused the life force or self with God, but still surrenders to the mysterious darkness. Hence one's heart of hearts continues to pray and experiences the "wilderness" of the ever-greater God.

Those who obey because of inmost fidelity to conscience, and not because of external necessity; who deny self and do their duty despite looking foolish in the eyes of others; who stand by their convictions regardless of the cost—they too are the mystics of daily life. Perhaps *the* mystical experience of daily life, for Rahner, is the courageous, total acceptance of life and of oneself when everything tangible seems to be collapsing. Anyone who has done this has at least implicitly accepted the holy Mystery which fills the emptiness of both life and oneself.[10]

3

Ignatian Prayer from a Woman's Perspective

Mary Garvin, S.N.J.M.

We gather together in this chapel on Halloween night, a night that has both religious and cultural origins, a night when children wearing masks stand at the door declaring: "Trick or treat!" Little girls' masks portray familiar women: Barbie—beautiful and seductive; the wicked Witch-symbol of danger and evil; and Super Mom—the woman who can do and be all things at all times. Throughout history women's reality has been equated with these masks. An early church father described the female sex: "What else is woman but a false friend, an inescapable punishment, a necessary evil, a natural temptation, a desirable calamity, a delectable detriment, an evil of nature painted with fair colors."[1] Women themselves believed these masks reflected their true identity.

What happens when women look into the mirror with their masks on? They, like others, mistake the mask for reality. A stereotype hides woman's true self and she becomes the mask she wears. It is like Marcel Marceau, the great French mime, portraying "The Mask Maker" as a gentle caring man creating the mask of a warrior. When the mask is finished, he puts it on and it gets stuck. He becomes the warrior.

Prayer is a time to take off the mask and to be face to face with God in all our truth. In this series on prayer we have been reflecting on these truths. Bill Barry reminded us that we can discover God in every human experience. Sebastian Moore helped us to recall that prayer is oneness of mind and heart in the presence of infinite mystery. Harvey Egan portrayed prayer as an opportunity to uproot our sinfulness and disorder (the masks, if you will) and find God's will as God communicates with us.

In this chapter we look at Ignatian prayer from *this* woman's perspective. I invite all of you to enter into this perspective, to reflect on Ignatian prayer and spirituality in our context as a university community trying to remain true to its Catholic Jesuit tradition.

I ask you, however, to remember the relatively recent presence of women in Jesuit higher education as students and as colleagues. So, first I invite women readers to explore the identity, mission and apostolic contribution of women in this context. I further invite them to confirm the importance of women's prayer and spirituality which urges us to take off the masks and reject the stereotypes inherited from historical, cultural and religious traditions. Let us come face to face with God as we are—women—our truest selves as persons in relationship with God, with one another, and with our world. We need to allow the truth, light and beauty of women's faces to reflect the image of God.

Then, I invite you men to be with us in this process and to take seriously and self-critically this new relationship of women and men in partnership and cooperation.

Now I want to focus on two points. First, to explore women's religious experience as a rich and valuable resource for a more complete understanding of prayer and spirituality. Second, to look at how Ignatian prayer and spirituality can be truly liberating for women.

Women and Spirituality

People are searching for spirituality, for a sense of connectedness to the holy. People want to contact the sacred no matter what their religion or culture. They are asking, "Who is God?" "How am I to be in relationship with God?" "What is the meaning of Life?" "Of suffering?" "Of death?" "How am I to be in the world, in *this* world, at *this* time?" "What is the path of holiness?" "How can we pray?" These are questions of persons on a spiritual journey.

Of course, these are not new questions. The whole Christian tradition speaks of this search for the holy and the meaning of life. The various traditions of Christian spirituality (Desert, Monastic, Franciscan, Dominican, Ignatian, etc.) have revealed insights into these questions. But an awareness of women's spiritual experience brings new questions to the search for holiness. Contemporary feminist spirituality rejects the aspects of religious tradition which assume that male experience and teaching should be normative for women. It also rejects the idea that the experience of prayer and spirituality is necessarily the same for women as for men. Moreover it rejects the assumption that men are to be the spiritual masters and women are to be the learners. The Christian feminist spirituality movement, influenced by the women's liberation movement, acknowledges the importance of the voices of theologians and of women at prayer to move this conversation forward.

In *New Catholic Women* Mary Jo Weaver defines spirituality as "faith made explicit in life." Spirituality encompasses one's deepest convictions with respect to the ultimate as they are embodied in relationships with others, with creation and with the divine. She goes on to say that traditional Catholic spirituality has a decidedly masculine character. Just as the "transcendent God mastered the chaos in order to create the world, so the spirit must master the flesh and the will must master desire in order to become obedient to a patriarchal God." Weaver goes on to say, "Just as feminists have found the Christian tradition to be inadequate in its language, its symbols and its theology, feminist spiritual writers decry the inability of traditional spirituality to reflect women's experience and provide women with a compelling inducement for their spiritual lives."[2]

Harvey Cox in *Turning East,* puts it another way.

> A male God creates a man who is supposedly led astray
> by a woman. There are male patriarchs and prophets, a
> male Christ and twelve male apostles, a male pope and
> bishops and priests. Women are either virgins or
> witches or whores or grateful child-bearers. There is
> obviously no place in this religion for a woman.[3]

David Tracy summarizes the issue in an article written in 1978.

> As sexism finally joins racism and classism as sins
> against our common humanity, and against the Chris-
> tian command to loving self-transcendence, we find that
> our own theological tradition is itself too often over-
> loaded, or even suffocated, with male language and
> male images of both God and humanity, with patriar-
> chal attitudes and practices in the institutional and in-
> terpersonal moments of our lives.[4]

Women, therefore, need religious models of prayer and spirituality with a positive view of woman, her gifts and contributions to
church and society. Women's ways of knowing and loving need
to be recognized. Women need affirmation of women's experience
as encompassing the whole person, body, mind and spirit, as the
place where they meet God in unique and personal ways. And
women need recognition and affirmation of women's ways of
identity and union through relationships, through care and connectedness to their own bodies, to other people, to the world and
to God.

Now let's listen to the prayer of two women expressing their
ways of holiness. First, a young girl, an adolescent awakening to
her identity as a woman with a sense of the goodness of the life
and beauty of the earth and the need for the community to care for
it.

> God, thank you for creating our world, and giving us a
> chance to live and grow. Too many of us take it for
> granted. God, you give us rainbows, and flowers, in a
> variety of color, and people, too, in a variety of cultures.
> But tomorrow all this beauty may be gone, if we don't
> take care. God, help us to realize that now is the time

to lend a hand, to take care of our earth and its people.
We can do it, I know we can. God, please help us.

The second is Consuela who says:

I experience God differently as one who experiences the
double oppression of being a woman and being poor.
God, give help and life to my own family, but especially
to orphans and widows who have so much suffering.
In my difficulty, give me strength, consistency, tenacity
and perseverance. Let me overcome my fear and fight
against suffering in silence. Drive out the demon that
makes me believe I'm worthless, I can't, I'm afraid, I
don't know. Break the bonds that enslave me and send
your spirit to make me free. Bridge the loneliness and
alienation I feel with the hope that community is possible and that your promise to those of us who believe in
you is true.[5]

Feminist spirituality questions the Christian tradition. What is
woman's experience of prayer? How does woman's body, mind
and heart affect her prayer? How are women taught to pray and
assess their prayer? Who are the authorities and experts on prayer?
How have male theologians, confessors and spiritual directors influenced women's spirituality and prayer? Who are the holy
women, and how do they pray? What stories of women in the tradition are held up as models of holiness for women and for men?

The complexity and the crisis behind such questions confronted
me when I attended a conference called "Women and Spirituality."
About five hundred women were present of diverse cultural and
economic experience: corporate lawyers, students, single parents
on welfare. Many had never affiliated with any church. Others,
however, had received their initial religious formation in either the
Jewish or Christian tradition, but were no longer active or partici-
pating members. Their experience convinced them that the system
and structures of their religions prevented rather than assisted
them in their spiritual quest. Religion, religious institutions, and
religious persons were, for them, obstacles to God. Yet, all these
women expressed a deep desire for spirituality. They affirmed the
beauty of the human person and of the earth as reflective of the
creative God. They desired healing for broken bodies and minds

and for the earth. They yearned for community. I was very troubled at this conference. I kept wondering, "Why isn't there any recognition, either in the workshop presentations or in the persons present, of Christian spirituality? Isn't there anything in our tradition that could contribute positively to this conversation?" Because of my own experience I asked myself, "Couldn't Ignatian spirituality speak a liberating word to these women who so obviously want more?"

Ignatian Spirituality

This question returns us to the focus of this chapter, a woman's perspective on Ignatian spirituality. This perspective has two aspects. First it is necessary to recognize and reject those aspects of Ignatian spirituality that deny or obscure women's truth. This perspective recognizes that the historical and cultural context in which Ignatius lived and the *Spiritual Exercises* were written was androcentric and expressed a certain bias against women. Then we will also look at those aspects of the Ignatian tradition that need to be reclaimed and renewed, aspects which strongly affirm and develop women's truth. This perspective of critique and confirmation examines first the text of the *Spiritual Exercises*, second the tradition or practice of the *Spiritual Exercises* and Jesuit spirituality and third the ways the *Spiritual Exercises* have been interpreted, taught and applied, the process of communicating the text and tradition to others. Therefore the key questions which face us are: How have the *Spiritual Exercises* been interpreted, taught and applied to women, how has Ignatian spirituality been formative for women? We will be asking: Where are women in the texts, the tradition and the teaching? How is women's experience relevant to critiquing and confirming the *Spiritual Exercises* and Ignatian spirituality?

Feminists remind us that women usually are invisible, or at least difficult to find. The history of religion usually excludes or ignores women. When we do find women, they very seldom speak for themselves and are often treated with either hostility or triviality. We begin by looking at aspects of the Ignatian spiritual tradition that seem to deny or at least obscure women's truth.

The Text: *Spiritual Exercises*

The index to the *Spiritual Exercises* has no references to women. But women familiar with the Exercises readily recall the image of a woman projected in the twelfth rule for the discernment of spirits for the First Week:

> The enemy conducts himself as a woman. He is a weakling before a show of strength, and a tyrant if he has his will. It is characteristic of a woman in a quarrel with a man to lose courage and take to flight if the man shows that he is determined and fearless. However, if the man loses courage and begins to flee, the anger, vindictiveness, and rage of the woman surge up and know no bounds. (N. 325)

In all fairness to Ignatius, we must recognize that he is only echoing attitudes of church fathers from earlier centuries. For example, St. John Chrysostom, Bishop of Constantinople at the close of the fourth century, warns male ascetics of his day of woman's corrupting power over men. It is like "taming a courageous lion," he says.

> Just as someone captures a proud and fiercely glaring lion, then shears his mane, breaks his teeth, clips his claws and renders him a disgraceful and ridiculous specimen, so that this fearsome and unassailable creature whose very roaring causes everyone to tremble is easily conquered even by children, so these women make all the men they capture easy for the devil to overcome. They render them softer, more hot-headed, shameful, mindless, irascible, insolent, importunate, ignoble, crude, servile, niggardly, reckless, nonsensical; and to sum it all up, the women take all their corrupting feminine customs and stamp them into the souls of men.[6]

Ignatius is not alone in equating masks with reality.

The text of the Exercises also contains images, examples, stories and scripture passages which are almost exclusively directed to male experience. Some references to images of God are: Lord, Divine Master, Eternal Lord, Father, King, Supreme Commmander, True Captain, Chief of the good, Christ the Lord. Some references to male experiences: Christian princes, three pairs of men, referring in the election to the choice between marriage and priesthood. Those familiar with the *Spiritual Exercises* recognize that there are few scripture passages highlighting women. Even the numerous references to Mary limit her name and identity to "Our Lady." Moreover, the presentation of the Two Standards assumes male experience when it speaks of the progression of temptation from riches to power to pride. Money, power and influence are not the usual position women find themselves in but rather poverty, powerlessness and self doubt.

Because of this meditation many people assume that this sinful progression is normative not only for men but also for women. Anne Carr, however, asserts that the opposite is true today for women.

> Christian writers have been inclined to speak of sin as pride, self-assertion and rebellion against God, and grace as the gift of self-sacrificial love. But in fact such categories relate more the experience of men in cultures that encourage them to roles of domination and power. Women's temptation, or 'sin,' conversely, relates lack of self assertion in relation to cultural and familial expectations, failure to assume responsibility to make choices for themselves, failure to discover their own personhood and uniqueness rather than finding their whole meaning in the too easy sacrifice of self for others. Reinterpreted by feminist theologians, grace takes on a wholly different character as the gift of claiming responsibility for one's life, as love of self as well as love of others, as the assumption of healthy power over one's life and circumstances.[7]

Tradition: Ignatius' Images and Experience

These are a few reflections on the text. Now let's look at two aspects of the tradition, the words and images used to communicate the Exercises and Ignatius' own experience with women. What do women associate with Jesuit tradition and prayer as it has been communicated to them through the years? Recently I led a workshop in New Zealand on apostolic spirituality. I asked the group of about one hundred women to give me some images for the spirituality of Ignatius of Loyola. Here is a representative sample of the responses. "Soldier." "Battle." "Military, fighting, war, conqueror, king, master." Their responses were consistent with the stories I have heard from many other women. They are also consistent with the words of a former Jesuit provincial who spoke of the "excruciating male and militaristic imagery of the *Spiritual Exercises.*" Perhaps the deeper question is: what impact do these images have on women and on men as well?

Now, let's listen for a moment to some stories of Ignatius and women. The stories of the founding persons of religious orders have a formative influence on the succeeding generations of members. Biographer Dalmasses describes Ignatius, prior to his conversion, this way. "Up to this time (his conversion), although very much attached to his faith he did not live in keeping with his belief or guard himself from sins; he was particularly careless about gambling, affairs with women, brawls, and the use of arms."[8] Did his prior "affairs with women" influence his later warning to his men that too great a familiarity with women could endanger their commitment and give scandal? In an undated letter to the Jesuits in Portugal, Ignatius writes:

> I would not have any dealings with young women of the common people, except in church, or in an open place. On the one hand, they are light-headed, and whether there be foundation for it or not, it frequently happens that such dealings give rise to evil talk. Such females are generally more inclined to be giddy and inconstant in God's service. After their devotions are over, they not infrequently turn, sometimes to the flesh, sometimes to fatigue. For this reason many allowances have to be made for their corporal needs."

He goes on to say:

> If I had to deal with women in matters spiritual, it would be with women of birth, whom no breath of evil rumor could arise. Above all I would not talk with any woman behind closed doors or in remote places. In this way I would avoid all criticism and suspicion.[9]

We know that these reservations and judgments are coming out of Ignatius' cultural context and experience; nevertheless this attitude perpetuates the image of woman as temptress and as morally weak.

Teaching

Now we come to the third dimension, the teaching and interpretation of the *Spiritual Exercises*. Many women who lived in religious life more than twenty years ago recall the obligatory yearly preached retreat led in a structured rigid form by a Jesuit director. He gave instructions and presented a uniform way of prayer. The only variation, often enough, came in the director's stories and examples. There was little, if any, awareness of the uniqueness of women's experience or women's needs.

After Vatican II, however, there was a growing awareness of the need for change. Jesuit George Ganss recognized that the Exercises were in considerable disfavor. There were murmurs, he says, and complaints. Ganss attributes the disfavor to ambiguous and confused terminology, inappropriate adaptation, discontent with lack of expected results. The form, the external structure of the Exercises was drawing too much attention to itself while the inner dynamism of the Exercises was being suffocated. The Exercises were not being adapted sufficiently to keep them effective in new circumstances.[10]

Now we come to our own day. Women are asking, "Is there anything of value for women in this text, in this tradition, in the teaching of Ignatian prayer and spirituality? Is this a text, tradition and teaching that is only for men and so dated and narrow that there is no current relevance? Why would a modern woman want to make the *Spiritual Exercises* which are so structured, so male, so Jesuit? What could they possibly say to a woman?

Rediscovery

Still women today who critique the text, Jesuit tradition and teaching discover not only elements to reject because they hide or distort women's truth, but a new perspective coming from their own experience of the *Spiritual Exercises* and Ignatian Spirituality and their insights into both. They are discovering a positive, affirming and liberating word for women. These last few pages will introduce this new perspective.

My own conviction that the Exercises do have a positive word for women comes from personal experience of making the Exercises over a thirty day period. To describe that experience to someone who has not made the full Exercises is like describing a Boston winter to a Southern Californian. In other words, to understand fully the Exercises one must experience them as a transformative experience for one's life.

I had a lot of anxiety as I began my thirty day retreat one January in Portland, Oregon. Moreover, I made the Exercises in a rather unusual context, a Jesuit novitiate. Hence I was doubly anxious. Would I fit into that structure and environment? How would I survive in an all male environment for thirty days?

The anxiety soon changed to appreciation as I discovered these thirty days to be a most liberating and confirming experience. The Exercises were uniquely adapted to my own life experience and to my vocation as a woman religious. I was very fortunate to have a wise, discerning, and creative director who saw his role as guide and companion in my own search and spiritual journey. The environment was part of the blessing. There was a strong sense of community even in the midst of silence, for I constantly felt the support and prayer of the Jesuit community. Basically, I discovered the dynamism of the *Spiritual Exercises* for a twentieth century American apostolic woman: God *is* faithful and active and deeply present to people.

My own experience has been confirmed as I have served as spiritual director and retreat leader for various individuals and for groups of women. I continue to be amazed at the uniqueness, the adaptability and the depth of Ignatius' vision. It is as relevant today as it was 450 years ago, perhaps even more so as it becomes more global and inclusive.

The Text Reclaimed

How can we look at the text with new eyes that release it from its cultural bias and stereotypes and enable it to speak to us today?

First we must beware of fundamentalism which would limit it to a literal and static interpretation. We must not forget that Ignatius composed the Exercises after years of refinement based on his own experience of giving the Exercises.

We now need to refocus attention and emphasis for our times. The text needs to be treated as a way of storytelling. I much prefer to think of the *Spiritual Exercises* as belonging to the oral tradition of the church. People of faith share their stories with one another and become transformed in the process. The experience of the Spiritual Exercises is telling and listening to stories, stories about the deepest questions we have as human beings, stories about life and its meaning, stories about death and its mystery. The stories are about who I am and who God is. The stories we relate reveal how this relationship develops and how it is blocked. These are stories of struggle and freedom in the life of Jesus and his disciples throughout history. The Exercises invite one into the dynamic power of story, with its images and symbols and its transformative power that reveals the deepest desires of our hearts, God's will for us.

The current surge of interest in spirituality and retreats reveals examples of women's search. One woman asked the basic religious question, "Who am I as a woman before God?" She describes her desire to enter into the experience of the *Spiritual Exercises*.

> I had a hunger for prayer, to know God and to be with God. I felt something was missing in my life. I felt a lot of different movements inside me and I needed time to sort them out. I had a desire to focus my emotions and life on what I consider to be important.[11]

Another woman took the text of the Principle and Foundation of the Exercises and rewrote it naming herself as subject.

> Woman is created to praise and reverence and serve God, and by this means to save her soul. And all the other things on the face of the earth are created for woman, that they might help her in attaining the end for which she is created. From this it follows that woman is to use them as much as they help her, and to rid herself of them so far as they hinder her.

The text is intended to engage the whole person. Ignatius envisioned the person at prayer as a unity; mind, heart, will, reason, feelings, body, environment, images and senses. The whole person comes to prayer. Any one of these aspects of the person or all of them become the vehicle for prayer. Memory and hope become a way to meet God since relationships with the entire universe and its people and their story are the "stuff" of Ignatian prayer.

The text also encourages the development of reflection and discernment so needed in our lives and in our world today. This ability to reflect, to move from a sense of silence and void to the value of attentiveness to one's inner life and listening to the voice of God in the silence, gives life a deeper meaning and invites one to respond. Prayerful reflection leads the way to discernment and the ability to recognize one's inner movements and their source and direction. Discernment can assist women to identify and claim personal responsibility for their own lives and decisions. Discernment helps us to distinguish between self-understanding and self-deception in ourselves and in the changing church and world. Effective ministry, relationships and personal ways of holiness and spirituality all depend on a discerning heart. Discernment leads one to draw from the source of truth which is within, one's inner sense of self-direction, rather than from external expectations of others based on cultural and historical stereotypes.

A new vision of the text of the *Spiritual Exercises* reveals them as powerful. To release this power, women and men need to bring their questions in faith to the experience of the Exercises and listen attentively to the response in their own heart. How do these scripture passages, these images, these stories, these themes and ways of prayer which are part of the *Spiritual Exercises* lead me to the truth that frees? Do I really believe in a personal God who loves me and desires to be in personal relationship with me as a woman, as a man, at this time, in this place, in these circumstances of my life? How deep and how strong is the desire within me to grow, to become more?

The Tradition Reclaimed

Finally, we look very briefly at the tradition by examining the life of Ignatius. One of his most significant practices was engaging in spiritual conversations, very often with women. Ignatius found in women people he could talk with about things that were very important to him. At one point in his autobiography he mentions that the only person he found to whom he could talk openly about his spiritual experiences was an old woman.

> Apart from his devotional practices, he employed himself in works of charity with the poor and sick. His chief apostolate was that of conversation, which won for him the goodwill of the people of Manresa. He was keen on finding persons with whom he might converse on spiritual topics. But he did not find them either at Manresa or Barcelona. There was only a devout old woman, known as a servant of God throughout the region, who after conversing with the Pilgrim of Manresa, said to him: "May it please our Lord Jesus Christ to appear to you someday."[12]

We also know that women assisted Ignatius in his apostolic endeavors, particularly in Rome. He established the House of St. Martha for reformed prostitutes and established a confraternity to provide housing for other "endangered" urban young women. He also gave time for spiritual renewal for women, particularly in the reform of convents.

But perhaps the situation that most reveals Ignatius in his relationships with women is his letter writing to women. These many letters are written with wisdom, direction and affection to significant women in his life. Writing to Sister Teresa Rejadella he says:

> It is true that for many years now, his Divine Majesty has given me the desire . . . to do everything I possibly can for all men and women who walk in his path of good will and pleasure, and in addition to serve those who work in his holy service.[13]

In the last 450 years many congregations of women religious have adapted the spirit and practice of the Ignatian vision as their foundational spirituality for apostolic women. In many cases until recently this apostolic orientation was deemed inappropriate for women. Society's expectations for the role of women indicated that the cloistered and monastic style were more fitting for the feminine character. Hence we have the dramatic story of Mary Ward who in the seventeenth century founded the English Ladies and established schools for girls modeled on the Jesuit schools for boys. Her sisters were animated by the vision and spirituality of Ignatius and received opposition from both Jesuits and non-Jesuits. Other visionary women throughout these centuries attempted to claim the inspiration of the *Spiritual Exercises* and the gifts of the Ignatian tradition for women. Another notable example is Thérèse Coudère, the nineteenth century foundress of the sisters of the Cenacle. She adapted the *Spiritual Exercises* and called it a new way of prayer for women. Her vision saw the significance of retreats for women and trained women to direct them.

The Teaching Renewed

The great church event of Vatican Council II brought the graces of renewal to the text and tradition of the *Spiritual Exercises* and a renewed teaching resulted. This renewal brought a return to the authentic sources of the Exercises. Both scholarship and practice led to new insights and applications of the Exercises for the contemporary world. The church experienced a new vitality and interest in the *Spiritual Exercises*. Retreat houses, renewal programs, parish and diocese renewal programs reflected this growing search for spirituality.

Now for the first time the teaching of the text and tradition was being done by women. Women schooled in the *Spiritual Exercises* and Ignatian Spirituality were providing leadership as retreat directors, spiritual directors and teachers. One example is a spiritual renewal program where seven hundred women have participated in "a retreat at home." Women directors gathered women in small groups for this retreat in daily life, based on Ignatius' suggestion in the nineteenth annotation. They call this the retreat of the future.[14] Women desiring a deeper spiritual life and more mature relationship with God find this need met in the *Spiritual Exercises* renewed for modern times and modern women. This religious experience rather than separating them from the challenges of life in the world, plunges them into it more with a deeper desire to find God in all things.

The words of one of our modern saints have special importance for women as we struggle to find a new place in our church and world. Archbishop Oscar Romero speaking of the impact of the Exercises on his life says:

> One cannot be separated from one's environment. Everyone is influenced by those causes, by those circumstances and must also be committed to changing those structures. If what retreatants seek is God's will in their lives, we can be sure that God will use each human life to redeem, to realize his design of salvation in the world.[15]

Conclusion

So on this Halloween, this eve of All Saints we remember those women and men who have walked before us on the pilgrim's path. We remember especially Ignatius and the vision he gave to the church, a vision which has been treasured by his companions and brothers in the Society of Jesus throughout the centuries. We also remember with hope those women and men who, inspired by this Ignatian vision, have lived lives of holiness because they searched and found God in all things.

Ignatian prayer and spirituality, particularly as experienced in the *Spiritual Exercises*, does have a liberating word to speak to women today. The dialogue between Christian feminism and Ignatian spirituality can reveal harmony and energy where insights and values converge as women's experience, struggles and gifts are recognized and affirmed. The convergence happens when women are aware of what binds them and as they seek freedom from his bondage. New insights are revealed when scripture and tradition are interpreted in response to the question, "What is the liberating word for women in this passage, story or example?" Women's energy grows when we recognize God's call within and trust it. It is that moment when women can be free to choose "more." One then realizes that the call to labor for the reign of God means a "co-laboration" directed to both women and men as a community of disciples and a prophetic presence in the world.

4

Ignatian Contemplation: The Use of Imagination in Prayer

William A. Barry, S.J.

Let's start very far from our topic. One of the great geniuses of
this century was Sigmund Freud. Have you ever wondered what
his core insight was? I believe that Freud's most original insight
from which most of the rest of his work stemmed was the realization that the most bizarre and irrational behavior, thoughts and
symptoms were meaningful. In other words, Freud had the insight that neurotic and psychotic symptoms and thoughts and be-
haviors had a psychological meaning, made sense, even though
they seemed totally nonsensical. Thus Freud tried to discover the
psychological meaning of dreams, slips of the tongue and pen, mo-
mentary forgetting. He considered *The Interpretation of Dreams* his
masterpiece, but he also wrote works entitled *Psychopathology of
Everyday Life*, which took up slips of tongue and pen, memory
lapses, and so on, and *Wit and Its Relation to the Unconscious*, which
developed a theory of the psychological meaning of jokes. In *Psychopathology of Everyday Life* Freud describes a rather amusing inci-
dent that occurred on a trip to Italy. He and a young man (who
was also Jewish) were discussing prejudice against Jews. The
young man was quite talented and ambitious and bemoaned the
fact that his generation would not be allowed to live up to their
potential. He wanted to conclude his passionate speech with a

quote from Dido's famous statement in Virgil's Aeneid "Exoriar(e) aliquis nostris ex ossibus ultor!" in which the unhappy Dido prays that an avenger will arise from her posterity to pay Aeneas back for loving and leaving her. But the young man couldn't get it right, and Freud helped him by giving him the correct quote, noting that he had forgotten the word "aliquis." The young man challenged Freud to show him how this lapse of memory had a meaning. Freud agreed to try but only on the condition that the other tell him everything that came to mind without censoring anything. In a fascinating page and a half the associations lead the young man to the point where he is embarrassed. He reveals that he is worried that he will hear that an Italian woman with whom he spent some time has missed her period. In other words, while passionately wanting, with Dido, posterity to avenge him, at the same time he does not want to hear that he will have posterity by this woman. The conflict led him to forget exactly that word, "aliquis," which, with its association to liquid and eventually to blood, would have reminded him of what he hoped would not happen. Freud's genius has led us to see that there is a psychological dimension to every human experience, that every human behavior no matter how bizarre or strange or irrational has psychological meaning.

Now we come closer to our topic. What was the original genial insight of Ignatius of Loyola? I would say that it was the idea that God can be found in all things, that every human experience has a religious dimension, has religious meaning. The point is illustrated in the very first chapter of the autobiography Ignatius dictated to Gonçalves da Càmara. Ignatius, the fiery, brave, womanizing, ambitious knight, was convalescing at the castle of Loyola from the shattering of his leg by a cannonball. Here is how Ignatius tells the story in the third person.

> As he was much given to reading worldly and fictitious books, usually called books of chivalry, when he felt better he asked to be given some of them to pass the time. But in that house none of those that he usually read could be found, so they gave him a Life of Christ and a book of the lives of the saints in Spanish.

> As he read them over many times, he became rather fond of what he found written there. Putting his read-

ing aside, he sometimes stopped to think about the things he had read and at other times about the things of the world that he used to think about before. Of the many vain things that presented themselves to him, one took such a hold on his heart that he was absorbed in thinking about it for two or three or four hours without realizing it: he imagined what he would do in the service of a certain lady, the means he would take so he could go to the country where she lived, the verses, the words he would say to her, the deeds of arms he would do in her service. He became so conceited with this that he did not consider how impossible it would be because the lady was not of the lower nobility nor a countess nor a duchess, but her station was higher than any of these.

Nevertheless, Our Lord assisted him, causing other thoughts that arose from the things he read to follow these. While reading the life of Our Lord and of the saints, he stopped to think, reasoning within himself, "What if I should do what St. Francis did, what St. Dominic did?" So he pondered over many things that he found to be good, always proposing to himself what was difficult and serious, and as he proposed them, they seemed to him easy to accomplish. But his every thought was to say to himself, "St. Dominic did this, therefore, I have to do it. St. Francis did this, therefore, I have to do it." These thoughts also lasted a good while, but when other matters intervened, the worldly thoughts mentioned above returned, and he also spent much time on them. This succession of such diverse thoughts, either of the worldly deeds he wished to achieve or of the deeds of God that came to his imagination, lasted for a long time, and he always dwelt at length on the thought before him, until he tired of it and put it aside and turned to other matters.

Yet there was this difference. When he was thinking about the things of the world, he took much delight in them, but afterwards, when he was tired and put them aside, he found that he was dry and discontented. But when he thought of going to Jerusalem, barefoot and eating nothing but herbs and undergoing all the other rigors that he saw the saints had endured, not only was he consoled when he had these thoughts, but even after putting them aside, he remained content and happy. He did not wonder, however, at this; nor did he stop to ponder the difference until one time his eyes were opened a little, and he began to marvel at the difference and to reflect upon it, realizing from experience that some thoughts left him sad and others happy. Little by little he came to recognize the difference between the spirits that agitated him, one from the demon, the other from God.[1]

I believe that this little story depicts the emergence of the core of Ignatian spirituality, that God can be found in all things. If God can be discovered in daydreams, then God can be found any-where. Just as Freud postulated that every human experience could be examined to discover its psychological meaning, so Igna-tius presumed that every human experience could be examined to discover its religious meaning. For Ignatius every human experi-ence, whatever else it is, is also an encounter with God, Father, Son and Holy Spirit. God is at every moment creating this universe and each creature in it and actively trying to draw every human being into community with God and one another. Thus God is, at every moment of our existence, in active, conscious relationship with the universe and with each one of us in particular. We are not, nor can we be, always conscious of God's presence drawing us into union with God, but we can become more conscious of that continual presence, if we want to. The *Spiritual Exercises* of Igna-tius are one of the ways of becoming more conscious of God's presence in our daily lives. Regular spiritual direction can also help us to become more conscious of God's action in our ordinary lives. Ignatius insisted that the daily examination of consciousness was a preeminent means of becoming more aware of God's contin-ual action. In the *Spiritual Exercises* Ignatius presents two sets of rules for the discernment of spirits. These rules are ways to dis-cover in our experience what is of God and what is not of God. Ignatius hopes that with these instructions and with the help of a spiritual director people can become contemplatives in action.

Near the end of his life Ignatius said that "whenever he wished, at whatever hour, he could find God." Ignatius was an extraordinarily busy man as the founder of a rapidly expanding order of apostolic men gradually scattered over the globe. He wrote thousands of letters during those years, founded a number of charitable institutions in Rome itself, wrote the Constitutions of the Society, met frequently with Popes, cardinals, bishops, and many others. He was no hermit in a cave alone with the alone, as it were. He probably led a life as busy as any of us. Yet he found God whenever he wished, he says. He became a contemplative in action. What this meant was that he kept meeting God all through his working day. Yet people found him very present to what was going on, present to their discussions, their feelings, their concerns. In other words, it was not as though he was spaced out, needing to be called back to the ordinary events before him. No, he was very present to the ordinary, and yet, if he is to be believed, found in the ordinary the extraordinary, found in the humdrum details of daily life Mystery itself. A contemplative in action in the Ignatian tradition is not someone who keeps walking into doors or walls, but someone who lives effectively in this world, yet still is never out of conscious touch with the Mystery we call God. In this essay I want to reflect on the way God used the imagination of Ignatius to lead him to become a contemplative in action.

Obviously Ignatius had a very strong imagination. He loved to read the romantic novels of his time that fired his own imagination to dream of doing great exploits for his king, his country and his "grande dame." He is not alone in this liking for romance, for heroic tales. Think of the popularity of the Western novel and movie in this country which enkindled the imaginations of countless people to imagine themselves as the hero or heroine bringing peace and justice to a harsh land. Think of the popularity of Tolkien's trilogy *The Lord of the Rings* in which wizards, elves, dwarves, human beings and hobbits (halflings) battle together to defeat the Dark Lord who threatens doom to the world. I have read the trilogy five times and each time tears come to my eyes when Frodo and the other hobbits are praised by the triumphant host for what they have accomplished to help defeat the Dark Lord. Aragorn, the King in the trilogy, is almost the exact image of the king used by Ignatius in his Kingdom meditation in the Exercises for he, too, shares all the toils and dangers of his men, leads them through the valley of the dead, and gives his all to save the world from the Dark Lord. Ignatius ate and drank such stories and they fired his ambition and desire to do great things.

God used this strong imagination to draw Ignatius to another kind of ambition. The gospel stories and the lives of saints are imaginative literature too. They can fire the imagination, and in Ignatius' case they did. You can imagine his distaste when these were the only books available in Loyola. But gradually they caught his interest, piqued his imagination, and the very same ambition which drove him to want to do great knightly deeds now takes over to have him imagine doing the same heroic deeds the saints did. And in Christ he finds a king to beat all imagined earthly kings. Finally he notices that the two sets of heroic imaginings have different repercussions in his heart. Ignatius discovered that the spirit of God was operative in both sets of imaginings, in the worldly imaginings to help him to taste the ultimate vanity of such exploits, and in the images of following Christ to help him to taste the lasting joy of being with Christ. Actually the way Ignatius uses the parable of the King to help fire up the imagination of the retreatant for the person of Jesus seems to have been the way the early Christians used the Suffering Servant stories of Isaiah to catch the imagination of their hearers. "Remember the story of the Suffering Servant in Isaiah! Well, in Jesus that story has come true, and in spades!"

Let me underline an important point here. Ignatius did not become a totally different person with this first discernment and his conversion. He was the same ambitious, driven man, but now he began to let God teach him gradually. He did not instantly become a man who easily discerned the will of God. Right after he left Loyola to take up his new life of following Jesus he and a Moor met on the road, both riding mules. They began to converse and the conversation turned to the topic of Mary, the mother of Jesus. The Moor could well imagine that Mary had conceived Jesus without benefit of a man, but he could not agree that she was a virgin after giving birth. Ignatius tried to dissuade him from this opinion, but could not succeed. The Autobiography tells us that the Moor raced on ahead of Ignatius, and we can imagine that he could feel Ignatius getting hot under the collar. Then Ignatius began to have misgivings about his behavior, that he had not done enough to uphold the honor of Our Lady. The desire came over him to race after the Moor and strike him with his dagger. He couldn't make up his mind. He couldn't discern what to do, in other words. And he was in an agony of indecision. Finally in desperation he decided to let the mule make the decision for him. He let the reins go slack. If the mule followed the broad road to the town to which the Moor was heading, Ignatius would seek him and strike him; if the mule kept to the road he was on, then he would let the Moor go. The mule kept to the road he was on. As you can see, Ignatius did not immediately become a master of discernment.[2]

From his own experience Ignatius learned how God could use his imaginative powers to teach him and draw him to a new way of life. We have already seen how the insight he gained from his daydreams during his convalescence was probably the kernel of the Kingdom meditation which he puts at the beginning of that part of the *Spiritual Exercises* given over to contemplating the public life of Jesus. It is aimed to fire the imagination with desire to know Jesus better in order to love him more and follow him more closely. But Ignatius also learned that God uses the gospel stories to draw us imaginatively into their world in order to reveal himself to us. So let us look at some of the suggestions Ignatius makes in the Exercises.

Let me use the two contemplations of the Incarnation and the Nativity. Here Ignatius spells out the suggestions that will apply for all the contemplations to come. In his suggestions for the contemplation of the incarnation we see how he let his imagination soar. The gospel text in Luke says, "In the sixth month, God sent the angel Gabriel to Nazareth, a town in Galilee . . ." (Lk. 1:26). Ignatius asks us to imagine the scene in heaven as the Trinity looked down on our world. What does God see and hear? Ignatius imagines the whole panorama of the world before the gaze of God, people of different races and cultures and customs, people doing all kinds of activities, but all in desperate need of help. God's response to all this is to decide to send the Word to become a human being. So the imagination shifts to the little, impoverished town of Nazareth and a young slip of a girl named Mary. Ignatius asks retreatants to imagine the scene, to hear what is said, notice what is happening, etc. The desire that Ignatius hopes retreatants will have as they contemplate this scene is that they might come to know Jesus more deeply in order to love him more and to follow him more closely. In other words, the desire is for a personal revelation of Jesus. Ignatius presupposes that God will use the imagination of retreatants to make this personal revelation of Jesus' values, loves, dreams and hopes, and his desires for each retreatant.

For the contemplation of the birth of Jesus Ignatius makes similar suggestions. In this case he encourages retreatants to become the servant of Mary and Joseph on the journey from Nazareth to Bethlehem. I have known people who have, in their imaginations, held the newborn Jesus in their arms. One pediatrician helped Mary with the birth itself. Again the purpose is to let God use our imaginations to help us to intimacy with Jesus.

After going into much detail in these two contemplations Ignatius leaves retreatants to their own creativity for most of the rest of the *Spiritual Exercises*. That was probably a wise move. The suggestions he makes in these two contemplations come from his own imagination. But our imaginations differ quite markedly. Some people have very vivid pictorial imaginations. They can, it seems, create an internal movie. I recall one man who went on a camping trip with Jesus for about five days of a thirty day retreat. Others have an auditory imagination. They carry on interior dialogues with God and with Jesus. Others, and here I include myself, seem to be unimaginative since they do not have these kinds of imagination. But I have learned that everyone has an imagination. If you wince when someone tells you about hitting himself on the thumb with a hammer, you have an imagination. If you can read a novel and enjoy it, you have an imagination. If you can recall the way you felt when you saw your first child as a baby, you have an imagination. By leaving retreatants to their own devices after the suggestions of the first two contemplations Ignatius avoids the mistake of making his own imagination the model for everyone else's. We need to let God use the imagination we have and not bemoan the fact that ours is different from other people's.

When we use our imaginations to contemplate the gospels, we expect that one of the influences on them will be God's Holy Spirit who dwells in our hearts. The Holy Spirit, however, is not the only influence on what happens. Ignatius speaks of the influence of the "enemy of human nature," the devil. In our own day we are aware that every human experience has multiple influences or determinants. Every human experience has a physical dimension because we are physical beings in a physical universe. The experience, in other words, is influenced by sun and moon, light and darkness, warmth and cold. Every human experience has a physiological dimension; we are influenced by what we have eaten and by our bodily functions. With Freud we know that every human experience is influenced by what has happened to us in our past that has left an imprint on our psyches. Culture and society also influence what and how we experience things and how we imagine. With all these influences on any experience we need to become discerning in order to distinguish what is of God from what is not from God. The rules for the discernment of spirits are helps to make such distinctions within our experience. In this essay we cannot go into that subject in great detail, but it may be helpful to take note of some of the basic principles of discernment.

Ignatian discernment first requires noticing what happens in our experience. Only after some time did Ignatius notice that the two sets of daydreams had different repercussions in his heart. Then Ignatius took seriously the differences and decided that the daydreams that left him happy and content afterwards were of God. One way, therefore, to tell what aspects of our experience are of God is to note what gives us inner contentment, long term happiness. Indeed, for someone who is sincerely trying to live a Christian life, Ignatius says, God's action brings an increase of contentment, of faith, hope and love, of inner peace. For such a person any inner movements or thoughts that bring inner disturbance, self-absorption, and discouragement are not of God. According to Ignatius God wants us to be deeply happy and contented. In this regard he is only echoing St. Paul in his letter to the Galatians. "But the fruit of the Spirit is love, joy, peace, patience, kindness, goodness, faithfulness, gentleness and self-control" (Gal. 5:22-23).[3]

Mention of the multiple influences on our imaginative contemplation of the gospels should not deter us from using this time-honored method of letting God reveal himself to us. Of course, we can fool ourselves or be fooled into taking for God's action what is only the result of indigestion or a psychic trauma. But if we avail ourselves of the help of a director or of someone to whom we can speak of our experiences, we can begin to tell the wheat from the chaff in our experience. In the process we will be on our way to becoming contemplatives in action, people who discover God's presence in our daily lives.

Part III

Development Through Prayer

In the history of spirituality there have been many attempts to describe the development of prayer. One describes development in terms of the three ways, the purgative, the illuminative and the unitive. Teresa of Avila speaks of the progression of rooms in the interior castle. Ignatius' *Spiritual Exercises* depicts the path of development during a thirty day retreat in terms of weeks. At a university one would expect that the development of prayer might be looked at from different angles. The next three chapters demonstrate this. Joseph Appleyard, S.J., English scholar and director of the Honors Program at B.C., looks at the development of prayer in terms of the stories we tell about ourselves. The psychologist of religion, Margaret Gorman, R.S.C.J., of the theology department describes the way the image of God changes throughout a life of prayer. John McDargh of the theology department uses the lens provided by psychoanalysis to examine the development of prayer and illustrates his thesis through the diaries of Etty Hillesum.

5

Prayer and the Stories We Use to Imagine Our Lives

J. A. Appleyard, S.J.

After all the different ways of looking at prayer we have seen, I thought it might be useful to consider the possibility that we might pray in different ways at different periods in our lives. In other words, to look at prayer in terms of the stages of cognitive and affective and social development we go through from childhood to old age, and to see whether this might not provide a useful framework for many of the other things we've learned about prayer in this collection.

You may be familiar with James Fowler's work. He describes the growth of faith, especially religious faith, in terms of a series of developmental stages drawn primarily from Jean Piaget, which change significantly across the life-span of an individual.[1] Fowler's outline of these stages could easily serve as a framework for a discussion of prayer by itself, but I would like to try an approach that's closer to my own experience, to what I know best as a student and teacher of literature, and to the work I have been doing in recent years. For some time now I've been interested in readers' responses to stories, and especially in describing how these responses change as a reader develops psychologically, from early childhood to adulthood. I've also wondered whether it is possible to talk about spiritual development in terms of the stories we use to imagine our lives.

When did it first become possible to model ourselves on characters in stories, to imagine our lives being lived like those of people we have learned to know entirely from books? It seems to be a relatively modern phenomenon.

Flaubert's heroine Emma Bovary in the mid-19th century is surely one of the most vivid examples of a person seduced by the dream of having her own life resemble the beautiful lives of the women in the romances she had read as a schoolgirl. But Don Quixote much earlier had confessed to Sancho Panza that Amadis of Gaul, the hero of many 14th and 15th century adventure tales, was his own model and should be the ideal of everyone who aspired to knighthood and a life of chivalry; indeed, the frustration of attempting to imitate his model in an unchivalric age was what undermined Don Quixote's sanity.

Now, of course, Emma Bovary and Don Quixote are themselves literary characters, so perhaps it is not surprising that they are represented as imagining their lives in terms of literary models. But does not this account of Don Quixote sound curiously like the situation of the youthful Ignatius Loyola recovering from his war injuries? He would have preferred, he says in his *Autobiography*, to pass the time reading tales of chivalry but because he could find only lives of the saints and of Christ he soon began to fancy himself imitating them instead. He marks this as the starting point of his spiritual life.

Long before Cervantes, though, mythic precedents in stories and songs probably provided models for the dreams of young men and women. The modern prevalence of storytelling, reading, and narrative entertainment in so many forms (movies, television, and, of course, novels) can only have reinforced this inclination to envision ourselves and our ideals in terms of stories. René Girard, in his book *Deceit, Desire, and the Novel*, uses the term "triangular desire" to describe this situation. An image mediates between the desiring subject and the object of passion so strongly that the image seems to model the kind of life that will achieve the object of desire.

I would like to suggest that the particular expression of desire that we call prayer is always more or less "triangular," in Girard's sense, that our relationship to God is always mediated through models, explicit or implicit, which take the form of stories about the significance of our lives. These stories provide the framework on which we imagine our relationship to God.

Where do these stories come from? I think they come, first of all, from our earliest childhood, from nursery rhymes and games and songs, from the prayers we're taught and the explanations we're given. They come from the tales our parents read to us from illustrated books—Mother Goose and Dr. Seuss and Maurice Sendak. They come in the form of family history and anecdotes. They come out of the experience of going to church, listening to sermons, hearing the Bible stories. They come from all the comic strips and TV shows and movies we digest without even being aware of them, from all the books of juvenile adventure and adolescent romance we read. They come in the form of history and biography and art as we get older.

All this is an enormous matrix of meaning, the collective memory of the human race as our particular culture passes it on to us. Its shape is something we absorb simply by being alive.

What does children's experience of stories have to do with prayer? If you don't already believe it, I hope you will take my assurance that our involvement with the imaginative world of stories from the earliest months of our childhood is immense and immensely significant. Stories *model* our view of the world and of ourselves in it, in both senses of the word "model." That is to say, they *reflect* and record the way we imagine ourselves and the world. And they *articulate*, they give an intelligible shape to, the view we have of the world and ourselves. This means that our view of the world is organized in terms of stories and of roles we can imagine ourselves playing in them. The picture we have of God and the way we imagine our relationship to God will depend on the stories which model our view of the world. We pray as we can imagine the plots and characters and themes of our lives. That is why I mentioned Girard's notion of "triangular desire": some image always mediates between us and the object of our desire. That image comes from a story or is a story. Let me try to make this claim plausible.

I have said that from many sources we accumulate an enormous matrix of meaning, whose shape we absorb simply by being alive. Some writers, especially those influenced by Freud and Jung, have tried to detect the patterns in this mass of material. They have suggested that there is really only one story underlying all the variations which particular cultures have produced. Otto Rank and Lord Raglan earlier in this century, and Joseph Campbell more recently, have outlined the primary myth of the hero—the figure of mysterious birth, who is tested in some kind of a contest against evil, returns with treasure or a healing boon, and achieves recognition and honor as a result.

I want to argue, however, that there is not just one story but four, and that the story of the hero is only the first and simplest of the four stories we are likely to learn as children. These four may ultimately compose one connected story, but it is more useful, at least as we begin this discussion, to envision them as four different stories, which we discover in turn as we grow up.

I am depending fairly closely here on Northrop Frye's description of what is characteristic about each of these stories. Frye sets out these descriptions in his pioneering work, *The Anatomy of Criticism*, an ambitious attempt to explicate the key patterns among all the plots, characters, motifs and themes of the immense body of literature which has constituted the Western European cultural heritage.[2] Frye discovers in this literature four generic modes of storytelling: romance, tragedy, irony and its companion satire, and comedy. Each of these modes has its characteristic settings, motifs, themes, and roles it allows to characters, and at bottom each depends on a particular view of life and its possibilities. The generic modes can be mixed together, of course, as in tragic comedy or satiric romance, but for the sake of achieving a clear typology I shall keep them separate.

I. Romance

The first of these generic stories is romance. What qualifies as a romance? You all know the story of *The Wizard of Oz*, though you probably know it from the 1939 MGM movie rather than from the book which L. Frank Baum published in 1900, and which has become the all-time American bestseller among children's books. It is the story of the orphan Dorothy. She and her dog Toto are carried by a cyclone from her aunt and uncle's dusty Kansas farm to the flowery green landscape of the Munchkins in the land of Oz. There, with the magic shoes from the good witch Glinda on her feet, she sets out for the Emerald City, in the company of the Scarecrow, the Tin Woodman and the Cowardly Lion. Each of these characters wants to obtain something from the great Wizard there, and when, after scary adventures with the forces of the Wicked Witch of the West they arrive at Oz, they discover that the Wizard is a fraud and that all along they have had the power themselves to make their own deepest wishes come true. In a marvelous balloon Dorothy leaves Oz and wakes up again in Kansas, surrounded by her aunt and uncle and her friends from the farm. At least that is the movie version.

What makes this a "romance"? I would start with the term "adventure." Think of all the stories in which characters face danger and resourcefully come through it. Then there are the fantasies which involve journeys to other worlds and heroic deeds there in order to return victoriously. But even books which involve no exotic settings or crimes solved or heroic fantasy turn out, nonetheless, to be adventures. E. B. White's *Charlotte's Web,* for example, is about a year in the life of a pig and a spider and a little farm girl, but its theme is danger faced and overcome.

Virtually all the fiction children read between the ages of 7 and 12 falls into this category. These are often very simply constructed stories, with uncomplicated sentences, short paragraphs, little description of people and settings, and almost no attention to the inner lives of the characters. The focus is heavily on dialogue and fast-moving action. The plot is apt to consist of a series of adventurous episodes, sometimes quite repetitive, punctuated by suspenseful climaxes, which eventually lead to a decisive confrontation. Often the link between episodes is nothing more than a simple "And then. . . ." Characters tend to be ideal types of good and bad persons, tagged with easily recognizable traits, which are mentioned whenever they appear in the story.

Simple though these stories are in construction, they employ an astonishing repertory of motifs drawn from legends and folk stories and the most ancient tales in world literature. Consider, for example, the exotic settings we frequently find in these stories ("long ago," "far away," an ancient kingdom, a great forest, a foreign country, a ranch out West, an abandoned mine, a house on a wild moor). Or the supernatural agents who make these stories work (witches, wizards, fairies, angels, wise elders). Or the anthropomorphized animals (dragons, trolls, elves, talking birds and fish, intelligent pets), the magic talismans (rings, amulets, shoes, jewels) and weapons (specially forged swords, laser guns, death rays), and special verbal forms (riddles, spells, curses, codes, warnings). The array of these ancient motifs or their contemporary equivalents should tip us off that we are not dealing here simply with bedtime stories for restless children. Much adult reading falls into this category too. Romance, indeed, seems to correspond to something fundamental in human experience.

Northrop Frye says that romance is the nearest of all literary forms to the wish-fulfilment dream. It pictures an ideal world where adventures always end happily. True enough, but this formula does not quite get at the special importance of romance. It is the literary form, Frye says, which deals with "the search of the libido or desiring self for a fulfillment that will deliver it from the anxieties of reality but will still contain that reality."[3] This way of putting it allows us to formulate the double function of the adventure story in the eyes of the reader: to give concrete form to threatening evil and then to assure that it will be defeated.

Why is this so crucial in the stories read by children when they are 7-12 years old? The answer perhaps lies in the developmental challenges which a child faces at this age. A vivid example is going to school. The child leaves the known world of family and home, and enters a wider social world of peers and non-familial adults, where he or she is offered systematic instruction in the language and numbers which Erik Erikson calls the "technology" of the culture.[4] School thus responds to the child's new and speeded-up cognitive capacity to gather and organize information and to the new curiosity about the world beyond immediate experience which for Piaget characterizes development in the years from 7 to 12 or so.

The growth of peer culture is another way in which the setting of childhood changes. As the child grows older, close friends, "the gang," become an alternative to the family, as a milieu in which a child can learn the collective informal wisdom of the culture and the rules of social relationships as the world beyond the family practices them, a milieu in which can be practiced the skills and competences that a newly enfranchised cultural apprentice needs to acquire.

The task of facing the challenges which the culture presents to the school-age child is not simply a cognitive one, however. Like the whole enterprise of learning one's way in the adult world (the "journey" after all is the major motif of romance), it involves the fundamental question of whether the child will turn out to be competent and therefore successful, or defeated by fearful and evil forces. The continually reenacted victory of the heroes and heroines of juvenile narratives assures the young reader that the adventure of travelling into the world and meeting its challenges can have a happy ending.

A child of 11-12 is limited, however, in imagining how the conflict of good and evil can be resolved. Frye does not suggest that romance is a child-centered literary form, but he does propose that the four "generic" literary modes—romance, tragedy, irony-satire, and comedy—form a cycle of episodes in a total quest-myth, whose parts are: adventure and conflict (corresponding to romance), catastrophe (tragedy), demoralization in defeat (irony-satire), and restoration in triumph (comedy). To go beyond romance in this cycle, however, requires being able to imagine wishes and dreams ending in catastrophe and death (the point of view of tragedy), or the permanent discrepancy between dreams and the ambiguous reality of actual experience (the point of view of irony and satire), or the transformation of this limited world into a new community freed from the power of death to undo it (the point of view of comedy). Young children cannot imagine these possibilities; they are beyond their cognitive and affective capacities. They can certainly imagine evil people and bad actions and temporary failure (these are the staples of adventure stories), but they cannot imagine a good person whose life ends in failure (as tragedy does), or that good and evil might be inextricably mixed together (as irony and satire do). So they telescope the cycle, and attach the happy ending of comedy to the adventure and conflict of romance.

This may be why so much juvenile literature consists of adventure stories, and why romance in Frye's sense seems to be the first literary form children can grasp and reproduce. It suits the way they view the world. It is the simplest way of envisioning the relationship of good and evil: to acknowledge their conflict and assert the inevitable victory of good. Though children soon outgrow simpler versions of romance which put it this way, the function of romance does not change. Adults never tire of it. Frye would say that this is because it is an essential part of the full cycle of mythic analogues of human life.

What might prayer be like when someone pictures the world in terms of romance? I suspect that it is apt to be a monologue about promises and bargains, about ideals and failures in achieving them. From a romance viewpoint God is surely an awesome figure, one whose noble qualities compel our loyalty and admiration, one who created us and cares for us—like a parent perhaps but one whose authority and love are perceived across a distance. One might dream of doing great deeds as a follower of this God, in hope of being greatly rewarded, but one might find it easier to pray to the saints or to Mary, who are concrete embodiments of the possibility of living virtuously, human mediators more easily imagined because they are more like ourselves, especially when we fail to live up to our hopes. The idealism of this point of view might express itself in extreme generosity and self-sacrifice, in a determination to hold back nothing, in the "holy follies" we hear about in the lives of the saints. More likely the concreteness in this way of thinking might show up in the resolution to "follow the rules," in hope of God's reciprocal fairness. The romance view of the world is an exciting and vivid one, but it is limited by the single scenario it can imagine. In a sense those who take a romance view of the world can see themselves as characters in a story—the great story of God's creation of the world and God's dealings with the world—but they can only see themselves from *within* the story, as characters who can choose to follow wholeheartedly or to fail cravenly. Overcoming this egocentrism will take some maturing, which we can better relate to the generic form of story called tragedy.

II. Tragedy

Tragedy relies on a different view of the world from romance. It acknowledges the realization that romance might not offer an adequate image of life's possibilities, and that an originally heroic destiny can end in catastrophe.

When we look for sample tragedies we are apt to think of *Oedipus* or *Hamlet*, but how about a relatively contemporary work like Arthur Miller's *All My Sons*, about a successful businessman who out of love for his younger son keeps him out of World War II, only to have his older son die because of the defective plane parts he has sold the government and then the younger son turn against him as a war profiteer? Or perhaps William Golding's *Lord of the Flies*, in which the shipwrecked children quickly lose their innocence, divide into hostile groups, and fall to hunting and killing each other?

My own unlikely suggestion as a model tragedy is Erich Segal's hugely popular novel and film of a few years ago, *Love Story*. It is about preppy types at Harvard, a hockey player from a socially elite New England family and a girl from a working-class Italian family in Providence who dreams of studying piano composition with Nadia Boulanger in Paris. The plot could cynically be described as boy-meets-girl/girl-dies-of-cancer/life-goes-on. I nominate this story because I think tragedy is an adolescent discovery. Though we associate the term with some of the sublimest texts in world literature, the point of view of tragedy is a starkly simple one, that bad things happen to good people, and this is a discovery of adolescence.

If you doubt this, think of the prominence of illness and death in books popular with teenagers. Cancer is a staple (Richard Peck's *Something For Joey*, Barbara Conklin's *P.S.: I Love You*, Doris Lund's *Eric*, John Gunther's *Death Be Not Proud*, William Blinn's *Brian's Song*). So are suicide or its aftermath (Judith Guest's *Ordinary People*, Judy Blume's *Forever*), psychological disorders (Joanne Greenberg's *I Never Promised You A Rose Garden*, Flora R. Schreiber's *Sybil*, James Reach's *David and Lisa*), crippling accidents (John Knowles' *A Separate Peace*, E. G. Valens' *The Other Side of the Mountain*), murder and other violent crimes (Judy Blume's *Tiger Eyes*, S. E. Hinton's four books, *The Outsiders*, *Tex*, *Rumblefish*, and *That Was Then, This Is Now*).

Why should these dark themes be so prominent in adolescent literature? One reason is that teenage readers have discovered that the conventions of juvenile literature don't match the complexity of their new experience. The stories of boys and girls who are not good looking or popular at school, whose encounters with the opposite sex are embarrassing rather than romantic, who have alcoholic parents or no date on Saturday night, seem to portray accurately the teenagers' view of their world better than romances now do. Illness and death are only extreme versions of this whole side of adolescent experience.

Northrop Frye points out that, whereas romance deals with the ideal order where endings are happy, tragedy explores the limits of our power to make our wishes and dreams come true. Its central idea is that catastrophe and death can befall a heroic character. Tragic heroes and heroines begin nobly, but something (God, the gods, fate, accident, necessity, circumstance) reduces them, makes them mediators between us and it. Thus, tragedy is an imaginative attempt to balance our potential greatness with our perishable nature.

It is instructive to see how well some of the characteristics of tragedy fit the adolescent world view. Thus, says Frye, tragedy concentrates not on a social group, as comedy does, but on the single individual, who is somewhere between the divine and the "all too human."[5] It tends to oppose the isolated individual to the social structure, and one of our deepest fears that tragedy plays on is the terror of being excluded from the group, and therefore of being pathetic. The plight of the tragic figure is that, isolated, one may make the wrong choices and discover too late the shape of the life one has created for one's self in comparison with the potential one has forsaken. But there may be no right choice either. The two reductive formulas for tragedy—that it exhibits the omnipotence of external fate, or that it is a result of a violation of the moral law—are complementary, not antithetical, truths about the existential predicament of human life. If this sounds all too much like the picture we often have of adolescents—yearning to discover an authentic individuality, conceiving great ideals, agonizing over their relationships to others, burdened by a sense of fate beyond their control, wondering whether the life choices they make will be the right ones, aware of the seemingly inescapable ambivalence of their feelings—it may be because tragedy is the literary genre which suits the adolescent's realization that the "real" world is not the green world of romance but a much darker and more danger-ous place.

What is the basis for this picture of adolescence? Of all devel-opmental transitions, it is perhaps the least in need of defending as a distinctive stage. Its conventional features are well known even outside the pages of psychology books: sudden and erratic physi-cal growth, intensified sexuality, idealism that is often grandiose as well as naive, self-consciousness, romanticism, moodiness and am-bivalence, ambition and drive, rebellion and crisis. Any or all of these might be found in the boy and girl between 13 and 17.

A useful way of relating these phenomena, suggested by Law-rence Kohlberg and Carol Gilligan, is to see them as manifestations of one central phenomenon: the discovery of the subjective self and of subjective experience as something unique. A child age 7-12 has only an inchoate notion of self; it is "me" or "you," the specific person who perceives an objective reality and acts on it. The child can be aware of subjective feelings and thoughts, but experiences these as directly caused by objective things and events. An adoles-cent, on the other hand, experiences an inner self as the locus of unique feelings, opinions and thoughts, which can have a greater reality and importance than the objective events which occasion them. The inner self is seen as authentic, the outer self a social role to be played, an appearance put on for others.

The discovery of the subjective self is concomitant with an in-tensified emotionality, and often ambivalent and conflicting feelings; it seems to be the necessary conditon for aesthetic feeling, for the contemplative experience of nature, for religious mysticism and romantic love. The discovery of subjectivity and the relativ-ism of points of view can also lead to a sense of isolation and lone-liness in the young adolescent. But the sense of a divided self-hood, of a split between a secret, authentic inner self ("the me no-body knows") and a changing personality needed to deal with the outside world, need not be proof of alienation. It can also be viewed as an attempt to come to grips with a philosophical truth about existence—that inside and outside differ and can be at odds—and to lay the necessary dialectical foundation for subse-quent development.[6]

Piaget's account of adolescents' cognitive development complements this description of the discovery of the subjective self. Whereas the 7-12-year-old child reasons concretely (in terms of objects and their classes and their concrete relationships here and now), the young adolescent begins to reason in terms of the formal or logical relationships which exist among propositions about objects. Thus he or she is not limited to thinking about real objects, but can think hypothetically about possible things, and can deduce the consequences which the hypotheses imply. This opening up to the possible is what allows an adolescent to think about the future, to construct theories and ideological systems, to develop ideals, to understand others' points of view. Correlative with this is the ability to think about thinking, to reflect critically about one's own thoughts. This is the source of adolescent self-consciousness and introspection, of the egocentrism of much adolescent thinking, of the sense of discrepancy between one's authentic self and the roles one plays for an imagined audience.[7]

This may be why older teenagers so often say that they like certain books because "they make me think." When you ask them what this means, sometimes it appears to be simply that they are enjoying the novel experience of being aware of their own thoughts as they read. If they are more articulate about their reactions, it can mean that they enjoy reflecting about the story characters and their motives. This can eventually turn into thinking about the "meaning" of a story, about the author's "purpose" or about what the author "is trying to say." Often this is formulated in terms of an image of *depth*: the "deeper" meaning is somehow below the surface waiting to be discovered. The generalized significance of a story is often summed up as its "moral" or its "lesson," a metaphysical statement about the world and the way things are. But meanings conflict and have to be judged. The adolescent turns philosopher precisely because the world now seems to be a complex phenomenon. The gamble symbolized by tragedy, that one's destiny might turn out to be either good or evil, throws back on the adolescent the burden of wisely choosing.

What would prayer be like to someone whose view of the world is cast in terms of this double awareness of the human potential for both grandeur and suffering? The clue, I think, is less in the philosophical perspectives this realization might inspire than in the split between outwardness and inwardness which it signals. Prayer might at times express an adolescent's fascination with what Frank Clooney calls "the lovely Other," the beauty, the holiness, the attractiveness of a mysterious God. At other times it is likely to be an exploration of feelings and newly discovered meanings and intentions inside oneself, perhaps not so different from daydreaming, a search inside for clues to the conflicts between what others think and what the inward self feels and thinks. Riding on a divided view of the world, it is also apt to be characterized by extreme highs and lows of feeling. But precisely because it is so personalized, prayer from this perspective can readily envision a personal relationship with God—or perhaps more likely with the human Christ—and therefore is apt to be more dialogue than monologue, a hunger for an Other who will accept and affirm and reassure one unconditionally. I suspect too that the prayer of someone who is conscious of the tragic potential of his or her own life might be dominated by the awareness of having to choose ways of living— of risking and even gambling one's life—and also of being chosen, since one's vocation (whether in the strict or broad sense) is typically an issue at this point in one's development. The future and its possibilities now come under question, and what and whom to trust are crucial questions, with by no means certain answers. The negative side of prayer at this point in one's development is that it can turn into an ideological life-support system: God's role is to protect and reinforce attitudes which yield not an inch to the conflicts and uncertainties of life experience. Adolescent totalism is no stranger to religion, any more than to politics or social relationships. But ideally this kind of rigidity is self-limiting; clashes of feelings and ideas unsettle the ground and prepare it for the development of new styles of thinking and feeling about one's life. What do we replace this view of ourselves and our world with, as we grow older?

III. Irony

The third of Northrop Frye's generic modes of storytelling he calls irony and satire. I propose that this is the story of middle age. I am going to speak only of irony here, because I think the term indicates a point of view towards the world better than satire, which to me suggests particular literary strategies and forms, rather than a stance towards one's life experience. What kind of story is ironic?

You are all familiar with what literary critics call "stable irony," that is, when the author's intention to say one thing and mean another is obvious and the reader cannot possibly read the work successfully without reconstructing the meaning intended by the author. A familiar example would be Jonathan Swift's *A Modest Proposal*, which suggests solving the Irish population problem by raising children commercially to be eaten, or George Orwell's fable about totalitarian communism, *Animal Farm*.

Frye, however, is interested in what critics have called "unstable" or "general" irony. An example might be a novel like Ken Kesey's *One Flew Over the Cuckoo's Nest*, about McMurphy the sailor incarcerated in a mental hospital where he seems saner than any of his doctors and nurses (especialy Nurse Cratchett), who attempts to help his fellow patients grasp the possibilities of their own humanity, and who ends up lobotomized so that he will be a tranquil and cooperative patient. Or perhaps one of modernism's high points, Samuel Beckett's play *Waiting for Godot*, with its bleakly funny picture of four characters passing the time in endlessly circular conversation as they wait for something that may or may not happen and that may or may not mean something. Or perhaps any of the short stories of John Cheever or the novels of John Updike, which subject the failed relationships and lost idealisms of suburban life to mordant examination. Or how about the forty-year-old novel which has aleady made its way into survey courses in American literature, and which many of you can recite parts of from memory, J. D. Salinger's *Catcher in the Rye?*

Frye's brilliant insight into the nature of irony as a literary mode is that it is a parody of romance: the hero is all too human, subject to the ills of the world, rather than linked by magical power to a transcendent one; his quests remain unfulfilled or they are wrongheaded or aimless; and he grows old and dies. Unlike romance where wishes come true or tragedy where greatness may be undone by a flaw or by fate, irony reflects the permanent discrepancy between what is and what ought to be. In its typical settings—the city, the prison, the hospital, the madhouse, hells of various kinds—the good and the innocent are the victims of the unscrupulous and love more often thwarted than conquering. This is the generic plot which, Frye says, attempts to give form to the shifting ambiguities and complexities of unidealized existence.

Irony, I think, is apt to be the predominant tone of the stories that we tell about ourselves in middle-age. The view of the world implied by tragedy is that, if we choose correctly, we can succeed grandly or at very least fail nobly. It is a view that can sustain us through the early years of adulthood. But by the time we reach middle-age we have gone through too many life crises and transitions to be able to take so sanguine a view of our expectations. We are likely to have had our share of disappointments as well as joys, moments of achievement and moments where we have failed others or ourselves, illnesses of our own, the deaths of those close to us, problematic relationships with husbands or wives or children. We may have a sense of having gone down the wrong roads, of having lost our youthful certainties and of not having replaced them with any framework of beliefs we wholly trust. The future is by no means clear or bright. Or perhaps it is all too easily imaginable: we can foresee retirement, illness, aging, and it is not a pleasant prospect.

One reason our view of the world is troublesome to us in middle-age is that we have learned to deal with the real complexity of experience. Paradoxically, though we are apt to have become better at taking account of things in their multiplicity, and at realizing how fragile and provisional our grasp of them is, this sophistication is not very comforting to us. When we were younger we saw things in black-and-white. Things were clearly right or wrong, true or false. As we grew older we encountered—in college perhaps—opinions, values, and styles of behavior different from our own, in conflict with ours, and often in conflict among themselves—a vivid example of the experience Piaget calls "cognitive disequilibrium." We react to this confusing multiplicity at first by considering it wrong, or a matter of appearance only, or simply a temporary condition on the way to authoritative solutions. We take refuge in the notion that all these uncertain matters belong to the realm of "opinion," unlike those which belong to the realm of the *truly* objective and knowable, like science or religion. Eventually, however, we are forced to the conclusion that the relativism of knowledge is not just confined to some areas of our experience, but that we're always going to be making up our minds in situations where we have only partial evidence, or that we're the only ones with a firsthand view of the relevant data, or that the conclusions we come to are profoundly influenced by the assumptions we start out with. What saves us from this crisis is the concomitant discovery that there are meaningful patterns and regularities in the evidence, that data can be related to the context in which they occur, that interpretations can be compared and evaluated, and that we become more and more skilled in arriving at plausible and defensible conclusions about what we know.

Though this process begins in the years of late adolescence and early maturity, and can be identified preeminently with college education in most peoples' lives, it seems likely that the work of adjusting to a relativistic view of knowledge goes on into the adult years. But it isn't only changes in our cognitive functioning that condition our view of the world. Our social relationships change and make new and problematic demands on us. As mothers and fathers, or as sons and daughters, we know both success and failure. Friends flourish and suffer. Work may be frustrating as well as gratifying. Even if we get enjoyment out of work done, or children, or relationships with others, it is under the sword of time. Health may become questionable. Or external pressures force their way into our lives: political and economic crises, weather, accidents. In a variety of ways, the older we get the less confidence we have that our experience deserves either the optimistic interpretation of romance or the grandeur of tragedy. Life levels out into a series of small joys undercut by longer running sorrows, more suited to the mordant double vision of irony.

What is prayer like in this situation? I suspect that its primary note is often *ambiguity*—ambiguity about competing visions of the meaning of our experience, about the sincerity of our own intentions, even about the conviction that God is listening to us and cares. To middle-age belong, I think, all the accounts of long stretches in which prayer is largely the experience of the absence of God. This is likely to be a period when faith becomes a conscious preoccupation, and images of faith as a journey or a leap become personally meaningful. It may also be a period when people deliberately turn to counselors and spiritual directors for help in reviving or deepening their practice of prayer. We *think* a lot about our lives and try to make sense out of them. "Making sense" can be an important criterion of our faith experience at this stage. John Haughey, in *The Conspiracy of God*, talks about the point of view (and I am arguing that it is also a stage in our spiritual development) which tries to work out intellectually the beliefs on which one can ground one's faith.[8] It is an attitude, he says, which picks and chooses among the doctrines and theological points of view and religious practices and images which one finds nourishing and life-sustaining. This attitude is, we know, a source of much vexation to Roman authorities these days. I suspect its root is the capacity we develop in the middle-age of our lives (and perhaps collectively at certain times in our culture's evolution) to see too many sides of an issue, to see the value of *all* the competing claims for our assent, and the need therefore to think hard about them and to construct interpretations which will satisfy the convictions we have extracted painfully from our own experience. The positive side of this ambiguity is a much greater capacity for tolerance of others' points of view, an interest in learning from their religious experience, on the assumption that their wisdom is as hard-won as our own. Prayer may be easiest at this stage precisely when it is for *others*—our children, aging parents, friends who are in critical situations, the nameless suffering—or when it is a dialogue with others—the dead who have been dear to us, perhaps. Erikson says that the choice facing us at this stage in our development is between generativity and stagnation. Either we will negotiate the crisis of self-doubt and learn to care creatively and productively for a widening circle of objects—offspring, friends, work, the institutions which shape our human community—or we will give way to self-absorption, impoverished interpersonal relationships, and boredom with our lives. Our prayer here seems also to have the ambiguity of irony, poised between growth and decline.

IV. Comedy

When I suggest that the fourth of the generic modes of storytelling is comedy, and that its point of view represents a final stage of our spiritual development, I am not thinking of *Police Academy* movies or stand-up comedians on late-night TV, or at any rate I am not thinking *only* of these kinds of comedy.

An example of what I have in mind would be one of Shakespeare's dramatic comedies, an early one like *A Midsummer Night's Dream*, with its mistaken identities among the lovers, the burlesque scenes of the workmen rehearsing their play, the intersecting world of fairies and spirits, and the final dance in celebration of love's reconciliations. Or a late one like *The Winter's Tale*, with its story of jealousy and recrimination among the elders, and frustrated love among the young, ending in forgiveness and reunion and even the dead returned to life.

A less fantastical example, closer to our own temper, might be Ingemar Bergman's film of a number of years ago, *Wild Strawberries*. The film dramatizes the reminiscences of a 76-year-old professor as he journeys by car to the city where he is to receive an honorary doctorate. There are a number of vivid scenes. The professor recalls a dream of his own funeral procession. The journey is interrupted at the old summer house of his childhood where he can still pick strawberries. There is an auto accident along the road, a memory of a midsummer family celebration, a frightening dream of his final examination in medical school, then finally the doctoral ceremony at which he is honored for his life's work. At the end a scene of reconciliation with his daughter-in-law and his son. Scarcely a comedy in the conventional sense, the film fits none of our other categories either. It is closest perhaps to irony in its view of the events of the doctor's youth and middle life, but departs from it significantly in the way it records how he finally comes to terms with the achievements and failures of the life he has lived. How can we make sense out of this kind of story?

Northrop Frye says that comedy celebrates the social, the integration and reconciliation of the hero or heroine with society. Comedy is typically about relationships and roles—familial, political, sexual—which get temporarily blocked, but the obstructing and unreasonable characters are transformed and the happy ending celebrates a new society, often symbolized by a feast, a dance, or a marriage. The comic vision reconciles as many characters as possible in its final society, and celebrates the power of imagination to raise experience above the limits of time and space and to transform people and things into the desirable images we have of them. The most comprehensive comic vision embraces the limitations and follies of the world of experience but asserts faith in more powerful images of reconciliation, renewal or rebirth.

It is easy to see that romantic and social comedies fit this description, but what should we say about something like Bergman's film? The title of Albert Cook's study of comedy *The Dark Voyage and the Golden Mean* suggests an answer. Cook says that the journey of the hero towards a confrontation with good and evil which is likely to end with his defeat and death is the realm of the "wonderful"; its literary form is tragedy. The celebration of the social norm of the reasonable belongs to the realm of the "probable," whose literary form is comedy. But the serene, sublime comedy of the greatest writers (he mentions the Homer of the *Odyssey*, Dante, and the late Shakespeare) encompasses both tragic discord and comic rebirth in the point of view Cook ingeniously calls "the-wonderful-as-probable."[9] It is a perspective which comes only as the wisdom of maturity. "Age," Cook says, "is concerned with the wonderful because it stands near death, and with the probable because it can look back personally on the course of life. With the prospect of eternity, life in time appears ephemeral and evanescent, like a mirror . . . or a dream."[10] But the wonderful hope of sharing in the triumph of good still seems probable. That is the vision of comedy.

We can consider the comic view as the result of moving *beyond* the radical antinomies of irony; the painful discrepancy in the world of experience between what is and what ideally ought to be is obliterated by a vision of a world once again golden. Alternatively, we can think of the comic view as resulting from *retracing backwards* the path of our reading history from irony back through tragedy and romance to the childhood vision of an imaginary world in which we can safely play—recapitulating the gains of each stage of our development as readers into comedy's vision of the flawed but redeemable world. Moving in either direction completes the circle which these four generic plots form, for comedy is the link, which as play starts the reader into the cycle of symbolic forms through which we experience the world, and as integrating vision brings it to a close.

What is prayer like in this comic vision of the world? Here we have to rely on guessing and speculating rather than on describing our own experience, since few of us would say that we have dwelt long or permanently in this vision. Nonetheless there are clues. Some of them are traditional, for example, the mystics' descriptions of the "unitive" state, or of the experience of God in marriage imagery, or the culminating idea of *The Spiritual Exercises* that one can "find God in all things." But I would like to find language that is consisent with the psychological and literary point of view I have been taking up to now. One useful clue is the notion of play. Play isn't very important to some psychologists. For Freud it is a form of release, of mastering anxiety-provoking situations. For Piaget it is a way of practicing things we already know and of learning social rules, but to the extent that it involves imaginary content it is simply a distortion of reality. D. W. Winnicott, however, thinks that in fantasy play we recover the first childhood experiences we had of the fusion of our inner experience and the outer world.[11] And Erikson views play as a form of experimenting with our identities in the world; we construct model situations, he says, in which we relive the past, re-present the present, and reimagine the future.[12] From this point of view prayer might be seen as a kind of carefree reinventing of our relationship with God. Faced with the puzzle of connecting the "wonderful" with the "probable," we simply try out the possibility that they are the same, and experience the different forms in which the payoff comes: flashes of illumination, the sense of being "surprised by joy," the experience of being taken out of ourselves ("ek-stasy").

Some of the images that men and women have used to express being in the presence of God emphasize the awesomeness of the experience: a burning bush, lightning flashes, a great wind, falling to the ground. I suspect that, for most of us on this side of the unitive vision, this experience is intimately bound up with profoundly personal images. T. S. Eliot, in thinking about the sources of poetry, asks:

> Why, for all of us, out of all that we have heard, seen, felt, in a lifetime do certain images recur, charged with emotion, rather than others? The song of one bird, the leap of one fish, at a particular place and time, the scent of one flower, an old woman on a German mountain path, six ruffians seen through an open window playing cards at night at a small French railway junction where there was a water-mill: such memories may have sym-

bolic value, but of what we cannot tell, for they come to represent the depth of feelings into which we cannot peer.[13]

I would suggest that it is often through these kind of images that our deepest experiences of God in prayer occur. Our psychic lives are immensely complex, and certainly many of the images that constitute our religious experience are common ones we have derived from our religious upbringing, from church ritual, from the bible, and even, if Jung is right, from the deep well of the collective human experience of encounters with God. Images like water, voice, light, sacred place, song, sacrifice, temple, sharing food, dancing, feast, cross, incense, vestments, and so forth. But I suspect that our mature experiences of God are wrapped up in the most intensely personal images—"charged with emotion," as Eliot says—that emphasize the continuity of the small events of our daily lives and God's great action in our world.

One of the oddest of these that I know of is the one that suddenly appears at the end of Dostoevsky's great novel about whether religious faith is possible in the wake of the Enlightenment, *The Brothers Karamazov*. The trial is over, the fates of the three brothers have been disclosed, and the final chapter of the long book turns unexpectedly to the funeral of a figure who has had nothing to do with the main story, little Ilyusha whom the other boys in the town made fun of and threw stones at because his father was poor and odd. The boys have befriended him again at Alexei's urging, and have kept him company through his illness and death. Now that he is buried, they are going back for a meal together. "It's all so strange," says one of the boys, "Such sorrow and all of a sudden pancakes...!" And then a moment later: "Is it really true that, as our religion tells us, we shall all rise from the dead and come to life and see one another again, all, and Ilyusha?" "Certainly," says Alexei in almost the last line of the novel, and "don't let it worry you that we shall be eating pancakes. It's a very old custom." I don't know where Dostoevsky got this image of pancakes, but John's gospel is a crucial source of the themes in the novel, and you may recall that John—or at any rate a follower of his—put at the end of his gospel the story of the disciples' marvelous catch of fish by the sea of Tiberias and of Jesus cooking breakfast for them on the shore. And the disciples recognize him in this al fresco eucharist. Out of what experience did Dostoevsky connect pancakes with the heavenly banquet? Who can say?

I may seem to be somewhat at a distance from the topic of prayer. If so, it is because I find it easier to speak indirectly about this kind of prayer out of the comic vision. I suspect it is really ineffable anyway. Three weeks before he died, William Butler Yeats wrote to a friend: "I am happy and I think full of an energy, of an energy I had despaired of. It seems to me that I have found what I wanted. When I try to put all into a phrase I say, 'Man can embody truth but he cannot know it.'"[14] Yeats liked the phrase "tragic joy" as a statement about his feelings in old age. Erikson refers to the "tragi-comedy" of aging, for he says that there is no total victory of integrity over despair, only a balance, if we are lucky, in integrity's favor.[15] He calls the point of view which holds the balance in place "faith," the adult version of the first and most basic human strength acquired in childhood, which he calls hope. Hope is the enduring belief in the attainability of our primal wishes, in spite of the dark urges and rages which mark our existence and threaten us with estrangement. The images which contain that hope may be the ones we have carried with us the longest, or they may be the prizes of our old age. The possibility of discovery is one of the motives which keeps us telling stories and listening to them.

6

Changing Images of God Throughout a Life of Prayer

Margaret Gorman, R.S.C.J.

Most of us recognize that our image of God has changed considerably since we were in grammar school. Such changes have always fascinated me. As a result of my interest in human development and especially in adult development I have done many interviews on faith development and have had my students also interview persons of different ages. Two key questions in any faith interview are these: "What is God like for you?" "What are you like for God?" The group I most like to interview are couples from the ages of thirty-five to fifty-five. I would like to begin with one of the best responses from these interviews as well with my experiences with two well-known psychologists, Abraham Maslow and Rollo May.

I interviewed one couple in which the husband was an agnostic astronomer and the wife a devout Methodist. The wife was concerned about Steve's agnosticism even though he was a good person. Clearly Steve did not want to be interviewed, and the opening minutes were rather stilted. Somewhat in desperation I said, "You must be impressed with the fact that you can predict where the stars will be." "Of course," he said, "the universe is not haphazard. It is not by chance, but I do not like your interventionist God." "Neither do I," I responded. "In fact, one of the greatest philosophers of the thirteenth century spoke of a primary cause and we are secondary causes." "Well, if you're talking about a primary cause, yes, I'll grant you, I believe in a primary cause. Now if you wish to label it God, so be it. I'll accept that, but, unfortunately, I grew up with the connotative meaning attached to that word as an interventionist."

We continued, and it became clear that he could not accept an image of a God which diminished human beings so that you pray rather than work on a problem. At the end of these interviews, I usually ask, "How do you pray?" In this instance I remember thinking to myself, "How am I going to ask him if he prays to a primary cause?" Then I decided to use Maslow's concept of peak experiences of oneness, truth, goodness, beauty, etc. So I asked, "Have you ever had a sense of oneness, beauty, etc.?"

He answered, "A sense of peace, definitely. Some of the most beautiful things that I can recollect occurred when I was alone with nature . . . like the night sky just before dawn." He went on and on about the "awesome beauty of nature." I asked, "Would you consider that praying?" "I suppose it could be because you are suddenly acknowledging the order of the universe, the beauty of it." "So you could be said to be prayerful?" "Yes." I told his wife that she need not worry about him.

My second example occurred when Abraham Maslow made one of his frequent visits to Newton College of the Sacred Heart at my invitation in the late 60's. I used to invite him over from Brandeis; his rewards were books by Teilhard de Chardin and others. He had always maintained that he was an atheist. This particular evening he had finished his talk to a large group of students when one of the most intelligent psychology majors asked him, "Doctor Maslow, you described those peak experiences with fourteen different adjectives, the one, true, good, beautiful, etc. Are they fourteen different beings or is there only being?" "Of course," said Maslow, "it is one being. In fact the qualities are interchangeable; the one is true, the true is good, etc. And I don't know what to call that being, so I call it 'Being X.'" At that point I said, "What you call 'Being X,' I call God." "Oh," said Maslow, "Father Van Kaam (then at Brandeis) always told me I was getting closer. Let me give you my history. My father was a nonbeliever; my mother was a compulsive ritualizer. We were always the first Jewish family on the block with Christians because we were so upwardly mobile. The only thing I knew about the Christian God was that he was worshipped by Christians who threw stones at Jews." So here is another example of someone who rejected his early view of God.

The last example is provided by Rollo May, the renowned psychologist who is also an ordained Lutheran minister. He was asked to speak on prayer and meditation at a meeting of the American Psychological Association's division 36, Psychologists Interested in Religious Issues. At the end of the talk to a very large audience, one member stood up and said, "You talk about that *thing* up there. What about some of us who do not believe in that *thing*?" May replied, "I do not believe it is *up there* but *in here*, and I cannot prove it to you, but that does not bother me a bit."

I give these examples to demonstrate what you have all observed, namely that believing adults usually form their own idea of God which may or may not conform to conventional views of God. Was it not Voltaire who said, "God made man to his own image and likeness, and man has returned the compliment?"

In *Philosophy of Symbolic Forms* Ernst Cassirer indicates that as human beings grew in their awareness of their selves, their image of God changed. In more primitive times they made the sun and moon into gods. Then as they became more self-reflective, they realized that living beings were of a higher order and so made gods of calves, bulls, etc. Further self-reflection made them realize that human beings were of a higher order than animals in the hierarchy of creation, and so the gods became super human beings, Jupiter, Apollo, Venus, etc. Finally they recognized that the highest power was invisible, a spirit, and the Israelites came to believe in the one God who is a spiritual presence. In our age with the rise of the theories of evolution and developmental psychology perhaps the image of an immutable God no longer speaks to our culture. Could this be the reason for the development of Process Theology with the image of God as process? The image of God is related to the culture to which it speaks. As we view ourselves as continually developing, so God must be in process. Of course, the reality of God cannot be enclosed in any one cultural image.

The link between one's understanding of one's self and one's self-image with one's image of God has recently been clarified by various psychologists, notably by Ana Maria Rizzuto and other object-relation theorists. Let's look briefly at Rizzuto's work and then examine in greater depth the developmental work of Robert Kegan. Both authors will, I believe, help us to recognize and understand how our image of God changes with our image of ourselves throughout the life-span.

The so-called object-relations school of psychoanalysis denies Freud's theory that neurosis is based on the repression of instincts. Rather, they believe, neurosis is the result of failed human relationships. In psychoanalytic theory "objects" are other persons. On the basis of experience with significant persons the child develops internal images of these persons ("objects"), especially of mother and father. These internal images are of relationships, of self in relation with these "objects." According to Rizzuto the child also develops an internal image of self in relation to God, perhaps containing all the idealized positive traits of the mother and/or father image.[1]

Another important concept in this school of developmental psychology is that of the "transitional object." This is something that a child uses for comfort and security as the child moves from one level of emotional development to another. A teddy bear, a security blanket or something like that becomes such a transitional object. The child goes to sleep with the object and feels secure upon awakening because that object helps him/her in the transition from waking to sleeping to waking.

For Rizzuto God is a special transitional object in that God is not made out of fabric but out of experiences with parents or other significant adults. However, while the child grows out of the need for the ordinary transitional object, he or she does not totally outgrow the need for the image of God. Sometimes we do not need the image, and it may be left in the corner for a while, especially if human relationships are going well. But when we face difficult times and become aware of our finiteness through failure, illness or the death of a loved one, we bring the image of God out of the corner where it has been neglected.

For Rizzuto, then, throughout life God remains a transitional object at the service of helping us to bear life's transitions. This is so, not so much because of God's own being, but because, like the teddy bear, the image of God has obtained a good half of its "stuffing" from the primary relationships the person has had in life. The other half of the God-image "stuffing" comes from the person's capacity to "create" a God according to his/her needs.

The psychic process of creating and finding God as such a transitional object never ceases in the course of life. It is a developmental process that goes on throughout the entire life cycle from birth to death. Rizzuto says: "If the God representation is not revised to keep pace with changes in self-representation, it soon becomes asychronous and is experienced as ridiculous or irrelevant or, on the contrary, threatening or dangerous."[2] Her central thesis is that God as a transitional object needs to be recreated in each developmental crisis if it is to be found relevant for lasting belief.

Rizzuto gives an interesting example to answer the question, "Does being theologically informed change one's God representation?" She recounts an encounter with a professor in the seminary who had a real conflict between the God of theology and the God of his prayer. When he spoke of the God of theology, he was pleasant looking, expansive and gracious. When he spoke of the God of his prayer and of his insomnia, he was tense, frowning and scared. Rizzuto told him that he was actually a polytheist who had two gods. She advised him to ask the God of his theology how he differed from the God of his prayers. When he followed her advice, a remarkable change occurred not only in his prayer life but in his general attitude to life, and his insomnia was cured.[3]

In another interesting report on the image of God Greeley found that 10% of the men and women he studied imaged God as mother. The correlates are fascinating. Men who have an image of God as mother pray more often and are more committed to social concerns. Men who report that their mothers or their spouses had a strong impact on their religious development are almost three times as likely to have an image of God as mother as those who do not report such maternal or spousal influence. Greeley concludes that the former men are more mature and that men may need the image of God as woman more than women do.[4] Thus there is evidence that early experiences with parents are important influences on the development of the image of God.

Rizzuto is a great help to understand our changing images of God, but I find even more helpful the model of development offered by Robert Kegan in *The Evolving Self*.[5] (Please look at Figure 1 to see a diagram of his developmental hypothesis.) Kegan hypothesizes two thrusts that lead to development of the person, the thrust to be autonomous or separate and the thrust to be connected or related or embedded. These two thrusts alternate in development as illustrated in Figure 1.

Infants are embedded in their impulses, but gradually they separate from this stage to see that they have their impulses and are their needs. Beginning with adolescence, persons see themselves as embedded in their relationships. By young adulthood many swing back to the autonomy pole and realize that they are no longer their relationships but have them. They have a sense of self-direction. The need for control and autonomy is there. I am my career, for example. But then comes the need to swing back to the pole of connectedness and we have the interindividual stage. The self has control and a career, but is not identified with either. There can be true interdependence with others and with God. So according to Kegan maturity is a process of balancing the tension between the yearning for inclusion and connectedness and the yearning for distinctiveness and autonomy.

I want to use this theory to speak of how our image of self in relation with God develops. (Please refer to Figure 2.) I propose that we are embedded in God as much as we are embedded in our impulses and needs, but we do not know it. Gradually, we separate ourselves from our impulses and needs and thus come to recognize them as something we have rather than are. In the process we get a clearer image of ourselves. So too, as we change our image of God, we get a clearer image or view of ourselves and of God. It follows that as our image of ourselves separates from false views of ourselves, so too does our image of God shift from false or inadequate views to truer images of God. We may have here a modern understanding of the purgative way of classical spirituality. Thus in Figure 2 I propose the parallel transformation of images of the self and images of God.

One further aspect needs to be considered. These psychological theories emphasize the person's work to develop a more adequate image of God. As psychological theories they quite rightly pre-

The Evolving Self

"I am finite, related
to the infinite"
(mid-life)

5. INTERINDIVIDUAL
"I have my career; I am
not my career—
commingling guaranteeing
distinct identities"
(mid-life, ages 25-   )

4. INSTITUTIONAL
"I no longer am my relationships;
I have relationships; I am my
institution; I govern myself"
(young adulthood, ages 18-25)

3. INTERPERSONAL
"I no longer am my needs;
I have needs: I am my
interpersonal relationships"
(adolescence, ages 11-18)

2. IMPERIAL
"I no longer am my impulses; I
have impulses; I am my needs,
desires, states"
(late childhood, ages 6-11)

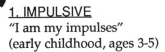

1. IMPULSIVE
"I am my impulses"
(early childhood, ages 3-5)

INCORPORATIVE
(infancy, ages 1-3)

Psychologies
favoring independence

Psychologies
favoring inclusion
(connectedness)

The Evolving Self

"I am finite
related, to
and rooted
in the infinite"

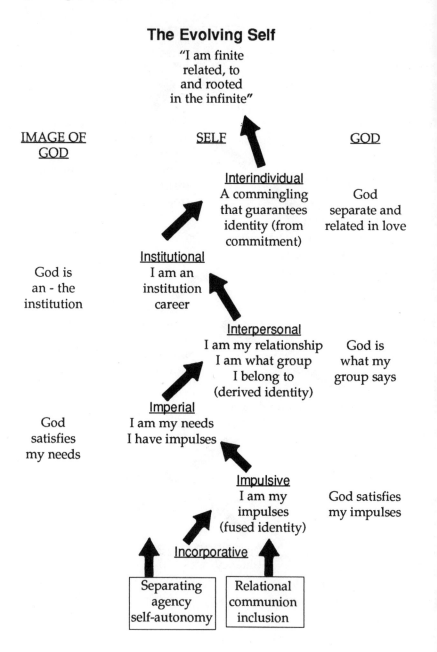

IMAGE OF
GOD
            SELF
            GOD

Interindividual
A commingling   God
that guarantees   separate and
identity (from   related in love
commitment)

God is   Institutional
an - the   I am an
institution   institution
         career

Interpersonal
I am my relationship   God is
I am what group   what my
I belong to   group says
(derived identity)

God   Imperial
satisfies   I am my needs
my needs   I have impulses

Impulsive
I am my   God satisfies
impulses   my impulses
(fused identity)

Incorporative

| Separating agency self-autonomy | Relational communion inclusion |

scind from God's work. But a believer holds that God is also operative in the process. Thus, for the believer there is a twofold process. As we grow in our awareness of ourselves, our image of God changes. But when God breaks in on us, God reveals more of God's self and of reality and thus changes our image of self in relation with God. Have you not emerged from a retreat or a prayer experience with a deep realization of God's love that has radically changed your image of yourself? What happens, for example, when we realize, as Sebastian Moore declares, that God desires us into existence as the apple of God's eye? Such a realization has to have a profound impact on our image of ourselves in relation with God. When we experience ourselves as sinners still loved and forgiven by God, has that experience not changed our image of God in relation to ourselves?

Karl Rahner gives examples of experiences of grace.

> Have we ever kept quiet even though we wanted to defend ourselves when we had been unfairly treated? Have we ever forgiven someone even though we got no thanks for it and our silent forgiveness was taken for granted? . . . Have we ever tried to love God when we are no longer being borne on the crest of the wave of enthusiastic feeling, when it is no longer possible to mistake our self and its vital urges for God?

He concludes that when we experience the spirit in this way, we have experienced the supernatural.[6]

I propose, therefore, that our image of God changes not only when we change our image of ourselves as the psychologists say, but also when God's presence is so keenly felt that we see ourselves differently in relationship to God. Thus we need to be alert and open to those experiences of our human finiteness, for often God breaks in then with love and strength. Loving God is not all on our side. We need to see that our love for God entails an openness to and acceptance of all signs of God's love for us. Our changing image of God is not all our work. God sees to that.

7

The Drama That Is Prayer: A Psychoanalytic Interpretation

John McDargh

At the beginning of virtually every lecture I have ever given—but in a special way now—I evoke the wisdom of one of my favorite theologians, the late Gracie Allen. Gracie used to say, "I have learned everything I know listening to myself talk about things I do not understand." Now that may seem the ultimate closed hermeneutical circle, but in fact it is quite insightful. What else is worth trying to talk about except those topics immense enough to "stand under," and how else do we learn how much there is still to know except by listening in to our stumbling efforts at understanding? This seems to me, as I said, especially the case when the thing I do not understand but am nevertheless continually compelled to try to talk about is the phenomenon called "prayer." I believe, with Frederich Heiler, that this activity named prayer is the "heart and center of all religion," and that "(n)ot in dogmas and institutions, not in rites and ethical ideals but in prayer do we grasp the peculiar quality of religious life."[1] And still I say that I do not understand it. This statement itself, I want you to appreciate, is historically remarkable, and if you can grasp why, you also understand something of the urgent motivations that get me to share my ignorance. Not so long ago for a Catholic theologian to have confessed that he did not understand prayer would have been at the very least an embarrassment. Who did not know what prayer was? After all we had whole manuals devoted to the subject. Prayer could be taught and it could be learned. There were experts and there were novices at it, but there was no great mystery about the whole business.

But I would suggest to you that whether we acknowledge it with regret or relief, today prayer has become profoundly problematic for a great many modern persons. At the same time, and for the same reasons, I am going to argue that prayer has also become more genuinely possible for modern or, perhaps we should say, for post-modern persons. The whole of my presentation will be devoted to exploring this problematic character of prayer and by pushing through it to uncover this emergent possibility.

I want to do this in three stages. First, I want to remind us briefly, if we need reminding, of some of the ways in which our own critical consciousness, as children of the Freudian revolution, renders prayer problematic. Then I am going to ask you to follow me into the discoveries and insights of post-Freudian, might we say, post-modern psychoanalytic practice and theory. These newer currents within psychoanalysis, identified with the "British school" of object-relations theory and American self-psychology, paint a rather different picture of the human being. With its central focus on the lifelong process of becoming a self, it is a picture that I believe opens the way for what I am terming a psychoanalytic *appreciation* of the meaning and value of prayer on its own terms. My choice of language is deliberate, for I am not arguing that contemporary psychoanalysis offers an apologia for prayer, let alone a legitimation. But it does, for me, open the way for a more profound understanding of the vicissitudes of the life of the spirit. Perhaps it will for you as well. But I do not want these reflections to remain simply abstract theorizing. As I was preparing this presentation, I felt the need to test these insights from contemporary psychoanalysis by bringing them to bear upon a real human life, to offer a case study in prayer. And since one of our persistent critiques of prayer is that it is an evasion of the trauma and tragedy of our age, I looked for a life in which prayer was discovered in the very midst of the conditions that seem to make it most im-

possible. Only such prayer I felt is credible to us who live under
the shadow of nuclear destruction or with the present devastation
of the AIDS epidemic. I believe that I have found such a life, and
in the last and longest section I want to bring the analytic perspective to bear upon the life of a 27 year old Dutch Jew, Etty
Hillesum. Etty's personal journal, kept between 1941 and 1943,
broken off by her own deportation to Auschwitz, was published
under the title *An Interrupted Life* in 1981 after having lain in obscu-
rity for some forty years.[2] I share the opinion of a number of other
writers in my field that her journal ranks with those of Simone
Weil and Dag Hammarskjold as a modern spiritual classic—perhaps even surpasses them. I shall let you make your own judg-
ment.

The Freudian Critique of Prayer

What then shall we say of the problematic character of prayer
for all of us who, whether we know it or not, do not look at the
world in the same way because of Freud? The awareness, indeed
the fear, that in prayer I may only be talking to myself, that is, that
there is no God who hears and answers prayer, is itself not new.
One could argue that it is indeed a very part of the experience of
prayer, as witness the psalmist's protest against the silence and apparent absence of God. What is new is the notion that prayer is
not talking to myself, but is in fact implicated in *an evasion of my
self*, that it represents at base an alienation from my own motives
and desires by projecting them outward. Not that there is no God,
but that the God of my address is my own creation, and that out of
my own most childish fears and needs. Again, the idea, as Freud
put it, that God created man in God's own image, and man returned the compliment, is not that original. Lucretius joked that if
horses had gods they surely would look like horses. What is novel
is the analysis of this constructive activity as neurotic, an enterprise of arrested development. The moral critique of prayer, at least
as old as Rousseau's Vicar of Savoy, is driven home in a new way
by Freud's hermeneutics of suspicion. Aware as we are that the
child is the parent of the adult, painfully aware of our capacity for
seemingly endless self-deception and of the complex web of our
motives known and unknown, conscious and unconscious, we can-

not but feel some appreciation for the chilly moral astringency of Freud's injunction that we labor for the withdrawal of projections and stoically learn to face the faceless universe without the compensating solace of a cosmic parent.

Where does this critique leave us? Analyzing this situation the French Cistercian, André Louf, arrives at a rather startling conclusion.

> We have lost the scent of prayer altogether. We are caught in the blind alley of an illusion. Many of us have touched zero point. Thank God! For now we can make a fresh start. . . . For this is the saving grace of our time, in the Church today: that we are now at our wit's end.[3]

For me help in making such a fresh start in the matter of prayer has arrived from a somewhat surprising direction. From within the psychoanalytic tradition itself. Not from Freud per se, but from succeeding generations of psychoanalytically informed researchers and theorists who carried Freud's method into other areas with other questions. In particular I am helped by that branch of the psychoanalytic diaspora that ended up in Great Britain and did things Freud never did, like actually work with troubled children, or observe the interactions of healthy parents and their infants, or think about the meaning for psychoanalytic theory of the experience of patients whose presenting complaint was not the hysterical symptomatology of the women who (as Erikson said) were "Freud's Gallapagos Island" but rather the complaint that they felt dead inside, cut off, isolated, without access to their own feelings and passions.[4]

The Contribution of the Neo-Psychoanalytic Movements

It would be an entirely separate presentation to sketch out the complex development of the psychoanalytic perspective upon which I shall be relying, but allow me to pull out a few elements most relevant for our discussion.

The work of analysts dealing with clients such as I have described converges with research into early infant development and work in ethology to frame a rather different picture of the human person than Freud had constructed. For Freud the essential motive force in human beings was described by the demand on the organism to maintain psychosomatic equilibration amidst the conflicting pressures of inner instinctual drives (primarily sex and aggression), and the demands of social reality (also internalized and exaggerated as the superego). By contrast, for theorists such as W. R. Fairbairn, D. W. Winnicott and others, the human being cannot be understood as an isolated and closed system of energies attempting to maintain itself. They and their colleagues were deeply impressed by the way in which the human infant is who she is by virtue of being born into a network of primal relationships toward which the child is essentially oriented for the recognition and acknowledgment that is being itself for the human person. Andras Angyal summarizes for me the thrust of these many theorists in a fashion poetic enough to be quoted in full.

> To be is to mean something to someone else. This existence we cannot directly create for ourselves; it can only be given to us by another. The true human problem is this: in a sense that matters to us above everything else, we are nothing in ourselves. All we have is a profound urge to exist and the dreadful experience of nonexistence. A poem written in a language that no one can read does not exist as a poem. Neither do we exist in a human sense until someone decodes us. A man in a most crucial way is a symbol, a message that comes to life only by being understood. Otherwise his existence has no more meaning or reality than an inscription on a rock on an uninhabited planet.[5]

During my recent sabbatical I did a clinical post-doctoral internship in a mental health clinic where I would say that a great many persons went through their lives with a pervasive feeling that they were inscriptions on rocks on an uninhabited planet—that no one had been there to understand and to decode them empathically, and that, in consequence and most tragically, they remained incomprehensible and locked away even to themselves. This is the understanding of human development that is the new and most promising growth on the tree of psychoanalysis. The essential tension in human living is not the conflict of instinctual drives, but the conflict between our profound intentionality towards communion, connection, affiliation and bonding—and our equally primary need to experience ourselves as separate centers of agency and creativity and potency. This formulation, which I borrow from Ernest Becker, is already a bit misleading, however, since it suggests the face off of two equal motive forces. In point of fact, because human beings are interpersonally oriented from the moment of birth, and because the child is only able to experience her own affectivity and agency in the context of the interpersonal environment, my own self-experience is always a function of the internal and external relationships which give me my sense of who I am and who I must be to be loved.

This sets up the theoretical framework which I want to bring to our analysis of prayer and, in particular, our examination of the "interrupted life" of Etty Hillesum. The British pediatrician and child analyst D. W. Winnicott formulated it as the problem of the true and false self.[6] In my own words this is the heart of the matter. Human beings are constituted from birth to experience a full range of affect and emotions, and are further oriented to approach the world—both the interpersonal world and the world of nature—as fledgling lovers, ready to take delight in giving delight to all that they encounter. My colleague Sebastian Moore calls this our "prethematic love affair with God." In any case, in the vicissitudes of the developmental process, our various lines of development: 1) the capacity to experience, express and identify our own affects, 2) our experience of ourselves as capable of inspiring and returning love, 3) our sense of our own competence to effect change in the world and in others—all will reflect the readiness of our interpersonal world to respond with empathy and understanding. In a word, to decode our need and to give it back to us. Little by little we come to a sense of self, woven of these recurrent patterns of action and response. The "false self dilemma" reflects the condition of unresponsiveness of that interpersonal world, so that in order to feel accepted and loved I must somehow deny or repress a dimension of my possible affective experience. Call that condition original sin, if you like, the fact is that all of us show up in various places along the schizoid continuum. All of us to varying degrees reflect in our self-experience the failure to be understood and the longing for that understanding as our original inheritance as human beings.

It is in the light of this analysis that I would begin to formulate a normative understanding of prayer. In a course I teach we work out some of the correlations between such an understanding and the insights of an ancient tradition of Christian spirituality which looks at prayer as precisely the uncovering and expression of the true self, the *imago Dei*. For the purposes of this presentation, a *psychoanalytic* appreciation, the consideration I bring is this: Is it possible that prayer can function in the healing of the schizoid splits in the personality so that it both sponsors and reflects the maturation of the person to a position of genuine interdependence? If one can document that process, then one has a compelling counter case to the classical Freudian depiction of prayer as arrested development. This is what I believe one finds in the life of Etty Hillesum, at least as disclosed in her journals and correspondence. Wary always of the dangers and limitations of doing a kind of psychobiography with such limited resources, nevertheless let us take the risks and pick up these psychoanalytic glasses to look at Etty and especially at Etty as a woman who learns how to pray.

The Interrupted and Yet Completed Life of Etty Hillesum

At the time we encounter Etty in her own journal she is a twenty-seven year old woman working on a degree in Slavic languages in Amsterdam and living in a lively and diverse household of older and younger persons of both Jewish and Christian backgrounds. The psychologically relevant facts of her family history must be gleaned from the lines, and sometimes from between the lines, of her journal and correspondence, but the outlines are fairly clear. Her family was a highly assimilated, non-observant family of intellectual, middle class Jews. In addition to Etty and her parents the family included two sons; Mischa, a high-strung and physically delicate young man whose brilliant early musical career as a concert pianist made him the center of family life, and Jaap, also a precocious intellect who made major biological discoveries at the age of seventeen and won early entrance into medical school. Etty's father was a classics scholar whose life revolved around his books and intellectual pursuits. He was the headmaster of a gymnasium in Deventer, Holland. Her mother was a Russian Jew who had fled during one of the numerous pogroms of the early twentieth century.

The values of the Hillesum family were fine, disciplined intellectual achievement; and its liabilities, a distinctive lack of competence in handling either emotions or the challenge of making commitments in a complex world. She writes of her parents:

> I think my parents felt out of their depth, and as life became more and more difficult they were gradually so overwhelmed that they became quite incapable of making up their minds about anything. They gave us children too much freedom of action and offered us nothing to cling on to. That was because they never established a foothold themselves.[7]

Only parents secure enough in their own sense of their personhood and their values can pass on to their children a secure internal sense that they can manage their lives and form their own values. Etty's father, though academically accomplished, lived in an atmosphere of vague intellectual abstractions and impractical philosophizing. Additionally he evoked continually from Etty a feeling of his emotional helplessness and dependency and made her feel that he could not be relied upon.

Etty's mother for her part was inconsistent, erratic and chaotic in her family life. She made constant demands on her family and her husband and seems to have spent a lot of time complaining about their inadequacy. Striking in Etty's descriptions of her mother is the theme of oral deprivation and greed. For Etty's mother, life was not a banquet but a ration line in which the limited goods of this world are distributed, but there is never enough. Etty describes in her journal the horror she once felt observing her mother eating "with utter abandon" at a banquet:

> Her gluttony gave her the air of being terrified of missing out on anything. There was something terribly pathetic about her as well as something bestially repulsive.

> That is how it seemed to me. In fact she was just an
> ordinary housewife in a blue lace dress eating her soup.
> If I could only fathom what I really felt deep down,
> why I observed her so closely, then I would understand
> a great deal about my mother. That fear of missing out
> on things makes you miss out on everything. Keeps
> you from reality.[8]

In this passage Etty shows herself aware that there is an element
of projection in her description of her mother, that what she must
really understand is her own sense of deprivation and desire to
grasp and hold on to life—which undoubtedly does originally de-
rive from features of her mother's relationship to her. The elements of Etty's false self linked to her relationship with both of her
parents are her fear of her own neediness and dependence (hence a
persona of self-sufficiency and stoic independence). As we shall
see, two growing lines in Etty's own spiritual development, realized in her experience of prayer and mediated in her significant
emotional relationships, will be her enlarging capacity to accept as
part of her self the little girl who wants to be held and comforted;
and a capacity to trust enough in the sufficiency of life's nurtur-
ance to let go. Note then these dual themes of dependence/inde-
pendence and holding on/letting go.

I want also to note another important theme in Etty's journal
which I think takes us into issues central to her experience of
prayer: the ambivalent role of language in the experience of the
self. In Etty's highly literate and competitive family, not food but
words were the staple of meaning and value, and so words were
what she clutched and collected. Her writing is, in part, an attempt in some sense to repossess language from her family so that
it might be a means of her own unique self expression. She has
some moments of stunning insight into this use of language:

> I think I know what all the "writing" was about as well:
> it was just another way of "owning," of drawing things
> tighter to oneself with words and images. And I'm sure
> that that used to be the very essence of my urge to
> write: I wanted to creep silently away from everyone
> with all my carefully hoarded treasure, to write it all
> down, keep tight hold of and have it all to myself.[9]

or again:

> Sometimes I want to flee with everything I possess into
> a few words, seek refuge in them. But there are still no
> words to shelter me. That is the real problem. I am in
> search of a haven, yet I must build it for myself stone by
> stone. Everyone seeks a home, a refuge. And I am al-
> ways in search of a few words.[10]

What Etty is in search of is a place where she can find her own
voice, a place where she can use language not out of the compulsive need finally to gain mastery, but freely, spontaneously, ex-
pressively—might we say, playfully. Eventually prayer becomes
such a place of play for her, a haven built "stone by stone" where
she can speak her heart without fear of the diminishment of self.
But that is getting ahead of our story. At the very beginning of the
journal, March 9, 1941, we meet a young woman who has been
traumatized by language, and the evidence for that is her distrust
of it, hence her proclivity to avoid a world mediated by language
for what seems safer and more manageable—the world of physical
relationship. Listen carefully:

> I am accomplished in bed, just about seasoned enough
> to be counted among the better lovers, and love does
> indeed suit me to perfection, and yet it remains a mere
> trifle, set apart from what is truly essential, and deep
> inside me something is still locked away. . . . I seem to
> be a match for most of life's problems, and yet deep
> down inside something like a tightly wound ball of
> twine binds me relentlessly, and at times I am nothing
> more or less than a miserable, frightened creature, de-
> spite the clarity with which I express myself.[11]

What an eloquent expression of the experience of the false self,
the disjuncture between surface and depth, between the compe-
tency of the social self able to be a match for most of life's problems, witty, articulate, and competent at love making—and yet
somehow cut off from a "more," a dimension of depth, a quality of
affect and desire unexpressed and unrealized. In this first entry is
the program and problem which occupies Etty for the remainder
of her short life—how to release the true self.

As one follows that process one is reminded of the truth of one of Freud's own dictums—that one cannot release one's self from the binds of illusion and neurosis. It is only in relationship that truth is revealed and healing happens. This was certainly the case for Etty. The beginning of her journal is virtually coincident with her meeting a man whose friendship was decisive in her own spiritual and psychological liberation. His name was Julius Speer, a Jewish refugee from Germany who had been encouraged by Carl Jung to pursue his study of psychochirology, the interpretation of personality by means of palm prints. Speer seems to have been a man of magnetic and charismatic personality, warm, energetic, intellectual. Etty went to him initially for therapy but soon became his Russian secretary, confident companion and eventually by very gradual stages his lover. Etty's early relationship partakes of many of the features of what might be called an idealizing transference. In a way that could never have been possible for her with her own feckless father, she is able in his presence to begin to experience her own long denied longing to be directed and taken care of. Note the way in which such an experience, while initially tied to the presence of Speer, begins to take hold and transform Etty so that the capacities she finds in herself become truly hers. She writes of her experience with Speer:

> He took me metaphorically by the hand and said, look, that's how you should live. All my life I had had the feeling that, for all my apparent self-reliance, if someone came along, took me by the hand and bothered about me, I would be only too willing and eager to deliver myself up to his care. . . . Suddenly I was living differently, more freely, more *flowingly*, the costive feeling vanished, a little calm and order came into my life, at first entirely under the influence of his magical personality, but gradually with the assent of my own psyche, of my own awareness.[12]

Etty herself is aware that her ability to live "flowingly," with a sense of inner freedom and spontaneity—we might say of playfulness—has a great deal to do with the holding environment afforded by the idealized "magical" person of Speer. But she is also aware of how this begins to generate a sense of inner self-assurance and security which enables her to stand on her own. We might recall here Heinz Kohut's notion of "transmuting internalizations." Evidence of how the relationship with Speer mediates to Etty a sense of the world as safe enough to be experienced and not grasped at is found in her description of an experience one night, fairly early in her association with Speer, as she bicycled home from an evening at his home:

> Whenever I saw a beautiful flower, what I longed to do was to press it to my heart, or eat it all up. It was more difficult with a piece of beautiful scenery, but the feeling was the same. . . . I was too sensual, I might almost write, too greedy. . . . But that night, only just gone, I reacted quite differently. I felt that God's world was beautiful despite everything, but its beauty now filled me with joy. I was just as deeply moved by that mysterious, still landscape in the dusk as I might have been before, but somehow I no longer wanted to own it. I went home invigorated and got back to work. And the scenery stayed with me, in the background, as a cloak about my soul, to put it poetically for once, but it no longer held me back: I no longer "masturbated with it."[13]

> And this grasping attitude, which is the best way I have of describing it, suddenly fell away from me. A thousand tyrannical chains were broken and I breathed freely again and felt strong and looked about with shining eyes. And now I don't want to own anything anymore and am free, now I suddenly own everything, now my inner riches are immeasurable.[14]

What is coming to birth in Etty is what we might term the capacity for contemplation—the ability to respond to the world in its "isness" without a need to distort it for defensive purposes. Allied with this is the distinction Etty herself comes slowly to make between what I would call the operation of fantasy and the work of the religious imagination. Because these processes are so crucial for this psychoanalytic appreciation of prayer I want to spend a moment on them.

Etty struggles with her awareness of the way in which a certain kind of compensatory fantasy, particularly what she called her "appetite for adventure and (my) far-ranging erotic curiosity" (p. 13), has served to insulate her from a satisfying contact with other persons, with the flow of life around her. She lectures herself rather ruthlessly:

> And that is something I have to learn and for which I must fight to the death: all fantasies and dreams shall be ejected by force from my brain and I shall sweep myself clean from within, to make space for real studies, large and small. To tell the truth I have never worked properly. It's the same with sex. If someone makes an impression on me, I can revel in erotic fantasies for days and nights on end. I don't think I ever realized how much energy that consumes, and how much it is bound to detract from real contact.[15]

I am reminded here of my colleague Robert Kegan's comment in his Harvard course on adolescent development, "the big problem with masturbation is that you don't meet many interesting people." Etty's awareness of the problematic function of fantasy goes further than this, however. She says to herself: "Your imagination and your emotions are like a vast ocean from which you wrest small pieces of land that might well be flooded again. That ocean is wide and elemental, but what matter are the small pieces of land you reclaim from it."[16]

One hears echoes here of Freud's image of analytic work as the dredging up and reclaiming of the Zuider Zee (an appropriate image for a Dutch woman), "where id is, there let ego be." For Etty what this means is the slow process of trying to attend, with patience and clarity, to what *is* and not what she wishes for, and a dedication to a process of trying to render that isness into words. Now at some level this participates in the Freudian ethic of a stoic renunciation of wishes, and the replacement of fantasy with a coolly "objective," not to say positivistic, account of life. But to read it only in those terms would be a mistake. More contemporary theorists such as Winnicott or the late Paul Pruyser offer us an alternative reading. What Etty is striving for here is to find a space in her life that is neither autistic, "untutored fantasy," nor the pared down naive positivism of "just the facts." To use Martin Buber's felicitous expression, she desires to "imagine the real."

And this, of course, is what she does. For her it means taking with equal seriousness both the events of her own interior life and to gaze with unflinching compassion on what is happening around her. At the same time she is quite aware that to really see what is requires an act of imaginative and empathic extension which first of all demands an intimacy with and compassion for her own inner life. As she writes: "To live fully outwardly and inwardly, not to ignore external reality for the sake of the inner life, or the reverse—that's quite a task."[17] Ultimately it is in the experience of prayer that Etty learns how to do this, and it is about her prayer that I want now to speak—though I hope it is clear that this is what we have been talking about all along.

It is the fact that her dear friend and mentor, Julius Speer, is himself a man of deep prayer that initially gives her the courage to attempt it. And not surprisingly, for a woman who has grown to distrust words, her first efforts at prayer are the risk of a physical gesture. Quite literally, she kneels down one night on a rough coconut husk mat on the floor of the untidy bathroom she shares with a house full of people. That gesture of kneeling, which she acknowledges is so foreign to her attenuated Jewish tradition, is, nevertheless, an act of tremendous psychic intimacy. She recognizes that in one important respect it is an exposure of the self more vulnerable than even at the moment of shared sexual passion. When she is compelled again to act, she writes:

> Last night, shortly before going to bed, I suddenly went down on my knees in the middle of this large room, between the steel chairs and the matting. Almost automatically. Forced to the ground by something stronger than myself. Sometime ago I said to myself, "you are a kneeler in training." I was still embarrassed by this act, as intimate as the gestures of love that cannot be put into words either, except by a poet.[18]

It takes her a longer time still to trust herself into the dialogues with God which she confides to her private journal. She thinks quite a bit about the courage it takes to say the name of God.

> Speer once said to me that it took quite a long time before he dared to say "God" without feeling that there was something ridiculous about it. Even though he was

a believer. And he said he prayed every night, prayed for others. And, shameless and brazen as always, wanting to know everything, I asked, "What exactly do you say when you pray?" And he was suddenly overcome with embarrassment, this man who always has clear, glass-bright answers to all my most searching and intimate questions, and he said shyly, "That I can not tell you. Not yet—later."[19]

Speer's reserve before this question is, of course, highly appropriate, for as Etty herself comes to realize—at its most genuine, the place of prayer is the place of the true self—that place where one risks one's point of inner poverty and indigence, as Merton called it, and allows oneself to be known. Etty speaks of this when she confesses into the privacy of her journal, "There is a really deep well inside me. And in it dwells God. Sometimes I am there too. But more often stones and grit block the well, and God is buried beneath. Then he must be dug out again too."[20]

I cannot help but be reminded of the comments of a Byzantine monk who was once asked how he reached the exceptional state of prayer that characterized his life. "Looking back," he said, "my impression is that for many, many years I was carrying prayer within my heart, but did not know it at the time. It was like a spring covered by a stone. Then at a certain moment Jesus took the stone away. At that the spring began to flow and has been flowing ever since."[21] For Etty, too, the place of prayer is not something outside of her, but a beyond that is within in which she holds, as she put it, "a silly, naive or deadly serious dialogue with what is deepest within me, which for convenience sake I call God." It is Speer who, I would propose, mediated the One who removed the stone from that spring in Etty's heart. But once the process began, it took on a life of its own, hesitant and always open to the chastening critique of a psychological consciousness, but progressively more certain of itself and its foundations in genuine affectivity.

But now I sometimes actually drop on my knees beside my bed, even on a cold winter night. And I listen in to myself, allow myself to be led, not by anything on the outside, but by what wells up from deep within. It's still no more than a beginning, I know. But it is no longer a shaky beginning, it has already taken root.[22]

This interior drama, this slow resurrection of the true self, this beginning to become rooted, is, of course, being played out against the backdrop of another greater drama to which Etty also remains fervently attentive: the systematic mass destruction of the Jewish population of Europe. For the Jewish population of the Netherlands it was a slow process of gradually diminishing personal freedoms and increasing limitations on all aspects of social, civil and economic life. Etty and her friends sit in a living room and enjoy a cup of the rationed and increasingly rare coffee and ponder the implications of the yellow stars they now must wear whenever they leave their homes. As I read the portrait painted in her journal of this slow suffering under the Nazi occupation, I could not but think of W.H. Auden's evocation of the insights of another Dutch artist, Brueghel, in the poem that begins:

> About suffering they were never wrong,
> The Old Masters: how well they understood
> Its human position; how it takes place
> While someone else is eating, or opening a window or
> just walking dully along. ("Musée des Beaux Arts.")

Such was the suffering recorded in Etty's journal. Around her, her old professors are arrested or commit suicide in despair, and every Dutch family has some tale of harassment or imprisonment, while life goes on and birthdays must be celebrated, and the blossoming of jasmine in the courtyard offers a solace unexplainable. When in February 1941 the Dutch people attempted the first strike against the Nazis in support of the Dutch Jews, the reaction is immediate and deadly. Jews are fired from jobs, ordered to liquidate assets, turn in jewelry and radios. Meanwhile Etty reads Rilke, and Jung and St. Augustine and every day the Gospel of Matthew. Another day the order comes out, no Jews on the trams. Signs appear in shop windows where Jewish families have traded for years: No Jews Allowed. Etty gives Russian lessons to young students, translates Dostoevsky and letters of Speer, worries about her parents off in the east of Holland, sleeps with Hans and sleeps with Speer, and prays. Parks are placed off limits. The countryside is forbidden to Jewish travelers. Leaving a pharmacy one can be accosted by a Dutch Christian who demands to know if one has been authorized to purchase tooth paste. And always in the background there are rumors of far worse things that are happening to the East, of labor camps and concentration camps and places in Poland with strange sounding names, like Oswiecim, or, as the Germans re-named it, Auschwitz.

Yet as the physical limitations on Etty's freedom draw tighter, her life as recorded in her journal seems to open up into a degree of inner freedom and lightness that is inexplicable to her and which she dares only share with her diary because it is so strange to her family and to many of her friends. She is herself initially suspicious of these moments of consolation and even of joy amidst the darkening clouds of the war, but discerns their authenticity precisely because she knows they do not withdraw her from the fate of her people.

> This morning I cycled along the Station Quay enjoying the broad sweep of the sky at the edge of the city and breathing in the fresh, unrationed air. And everywhere signs barring Jews from the paths and the open country. The sky within me is as wide as the one stretching above my head. I believe in God and I believe in man and I say so without embarrassment. Life is hard, but that is no bad thing. If one starts by taking one's own importance seriously, the rest follows. It is not morbid individualism to work on oneself. True peace will come only when every individual finds peace within himself; when we have all vanquished and transformed our hatred for our fellow human beings of whatever race— even into love one day, although that is perhaps asking too much. It is however the only solution. I am a happy person and I hold life dear indeed, in this year of Our Lord 1942, the umpteenth year of the war.[23]

For Etty, the temptation of the false self would have been to identify with the abstract idealism of her father and to disparage her own feelings and experience, to have given away her own self-experience because it really does not matter next to the suffering of another (even as in her home, one suspects, it did not matter compared to the loudly lamented sufferings of her mother, or the quiet despair of her father). But one cannot lose the self unless one has a self to lose, and the healing of Etty's life is to possess herself so completely that eventually and in time it can be laid down for others—not out of guilt, but out of generosity. Thus Etty comes to feel that she betrays her generation if she evades her own experience even with apparent nobility of motive. Hence she concludes at one point:

> With all the suffering there is, you begin to feel ashamed of taking yourself and your moods so seriously. But you must continue to take yourself seriously, you must remain your own witness, marking well everything that happens in this world, never shutting your eyes to reality. You must come to grips with these terrible times, and try to answer the many questions they pose. . . . I want to live to see the future, to become the chronicler of the things that are happening.[24]

After this entry Etty only lives to chronicle another year and a half of that future, but in that year she lives a lifetime. On June 29th, 1942 the terrible news finally arrives. The entire Jewish population of the Netherlands is to be deported through a holding camp called Westerbork and thence to Poland. She is under no illusion that this will be anything other than a one-way trip.

> I must admit a new insight into my life and find a place for it: what is at stake is our impending destruction and annihilation, we can have no illusions about that. They are out to destroy us completely. We must accept that and go on from there.[25]

One finds in Etty's journal her growing conviction that she has finally found a life of her own, one that makes sense. It is a profound sense of having a destiny, of having a role to play in an historical drama that fits her, that is self-chosen and uniquely hers, and it is precisely the role of being in solidarity with the Jewish people of the Netherlands, not as an abstraction, but in their tragic, messy, unedifying and holy particularity, and of telling that story.

> Ours is now a common destiny and that is something we must not forget. A very hard day. But I keep finding myself in prayer. And that is something I shall always be able to do, even in the smallest space. Pray. And that part of our common destiny which I must shoulder myself, I strap tightly and firmly to my back, it becomes part of me, as I walk through the streets even now.[26]

And she does shoulder that burden. On July 15, 1942, about the same time as a young girl named Anne Frank was beginning her own diary hidden in a warehouse a few miles away, Etty walks to the Headquarters of the Jewish Council, an organization set up to work with the Nazis to facilitate the deportation of the Jewish community, and begins to work as a typist. She thought initially that this might be one way of helping her people, but the experience is horrifying to her, Jews collaborating in the decision about who shall live and who shall die. And after only two weeks of working in what she described as something "between hell and a mad house," she voluntarily joined the first roundup of Jews being sent to Westerbork to work there as a social worker. She was determined to share the fate of her people in its depth. From August 1942 until September 1943 she worked in Westerbork, punctuated only by bouts of illness during which she was allowed to return to Amsterdam to recuperate. During that first month her beloved Julius Speer died suddenly of an illness. What she writes of him is revealing of his role in her life, and of the way in which she had moved through him and beyond to a new level of inner freedom. She addresses the departed Speer:

> What energies I possess have been set free inside me. You taught me to speak the name of God without embarrassment. You were the mediator between God and me, and now you, the mediator, have gone and my path leads straight to God. It is right that it should be so. And I shall be the mediator for any soul I can reach.[27]

The records that have reached us from persons who knew Etty in Westerbork describe a young woman who in the very midst of tremendous horror and pathos impressed persons as "luminous." They streamed into Westerbork from all over Holland: the paralyzed, and the insane, and the pregnant and ill, aristocrats and con men, children and the elderly, all Jews, but also hundreds of Catholic monks and nuns and priests of Jewish background rounded up for extermination in reprisal for the Dutch hierarchy's opposition to the Nazi occupation. In her journals and in her correspondence she attempted to fulfill what she lived out in her daily service to the suffering thousands whom she served, "to be the thinking heart of the barracks."[28] I wish that I could read to you from her account of life in Westerbork, but I could not bear to even had I time. In its portrayal of the smallest human details of that suffering it makes its enormity more vivid than all the statistics and figures one could digest. Since my focus has been upon the development of Etty as a person of prayer I wanted to say one last thing about that prayer that typified her last months in Westerbork.

The classical psychoanalytic critique of prayer rather uniformly characterizes prayer as petition for relief from suffering, rescue from distress, or some other form of cosmic assistance by a God postulated as possessing all the power we humans so clearly do not. Such a critique must fall silent before the very different experience of prayer recorded in Etty's journal. For what is most striking about that prayer is that it is addressed to a God whom Etty experiences as powerless to save and utterly vulnerable, yet faithfully identified with that which she knows to be truest about her own essential identity and that of every other human being. She speaks thus to God:

> I shall try to help You, God, to stop my strength ebbing away, though I cannot vouch for it in advance. But one thing is becoming increasingly clear to me: that You cannot help us, that we must help You to help ourselves. And that is all we can manage these days, and also all that really matters: that we safeguard that little piece of You, God, in ourselves. And perhaps in others as well. Alas, there doesn't seem to be much You Yourself can do about our circumstances, about our lives. Neither do I hold You responsible. You cannot help us but we must help You and defend Your dwelling place inside us to the end.[29]

Recently when I made a pilgrimage to Auschwitz and stood on the railroad siding, it was Etty's face and words which represented for me the unknown faces of the thousands of our people, Jews and gentile, gay men and women and Gypsies and prisoners of war who perished there. Etty, I am convinced you defended that dwelling place of God within to the very end, and because you did, like all the saints, you have made it more possible for us to believe that it can be done. Standing there I recalled the words you scratched out on a post card and threw from the train window as it left Holland. The post card was found by farmers outside the camp and posted by them. It read:

September 7, 1943

Opening the Bible at random I find this: "The Lord is my high tower." I am sitting on my ruck sack in the middle of a full freight train. Father, Mother and Mischa are a few cars away. In the end the departure came without warning. On sudden special orders from the Hague. We left the camp singing . . .[30]

Part IV

Prayer in Many Places

One of the more fascinating aspects of this series on prayer was the discovery of the various ways people prayed and of the variety of praying people. Some of the talks not produced in this volume took up topics as varied as the Eucharist as prayer, the liturgy of hours, journaling as prayer, prayer through gesture and dance, art as prayer, the poem as prayer, and praying the rosary. In this section we reproduce three presentations that indicate the variety of places where one can meet God and thus engage in prayer. Dennis J. Sardella, professor of chemistry, writes about science and prayer. Richard Carroll Keeley, director of the PULSE program at Boston College, develops the ancient Benedictine theme "Ora et labora" to show how work can become prayer. Finally, Francis X. Clooney, S.J., a scholar in Indian religions and professor in the theology department, demonstrates the possibility and the difficulties for a Christian to pray through the non-Christian.

8

Thoughts About Science and Prayer

Dennis J. Sardella

When I first started thinking about this presentation on Science and Prayer, I mentioned it to several friends, just to get their reactions, and the results were, to say the least, interesting! One friend—a priest—raised his eyebrows to an anatomically embarrassing height and said that there really was no connection—that they dealt with two entirely different things. Another—a scientist—just laughed and said "Good luck, you're going to need it!"

Both responses left me rather deflated, and wondering if I was about to pay the price for having an inflated ego. I began to confront the very real possibility that I was about to reveal my incompetence in *two* fields in the same presentation, a dubious achievement at best! For the first time I could really identify with how my wife felt in the advanced stages of labor as they wheeled her into the elevator of St. Margaret's Hospital for the birth of our first child. She said to me afterwards, "All I kept thinking was 'I don't want to do this, I want to go home', but I knew it was too late to back out."

Shortly afterwards, the first of several friends confronted me excitedly and said she was really looking forward to hearing what I had to say, to which my reaction was (and still is) "So am I!"

It's easier for me to tell you what I'm *not* going to talk about, than what I *am* going to say. I'm not going to try to convince you that if you pray over your plants, they'll grow better (they may), or that you can prove (or disprove) the existence of God from thermodynamics, or quantum mechanics, or the periodic table, or evolution. In fact, I'm not going to talk about apologetics at all, because I'm not sure what—if anything—science can tell us directly about God. Someone supposedly once asked the great British biologist J.B.S. Haldane what he thought one could learn about the Almighty from the study of biology, to which Haldane replied, "Nothing, other than that he seems inordinately fond of beetles." (I should mention that there are some 50,000 species of beetles in the world.)

What, in fact, I want to do here is to focus less on science and prayer and more on some principles that I think are common to scientists and people who pray, since I consider myself to be a member of both groups. I hope to suggest to you that science and prayer are not necessarily totally different, or mutually exclusive, but complementary. As part of this exploration, I want to look at some principles of science, and at the inner motivations of scientists.

Let's begin by asking what makes a scientist. Scientists are curious, but it seems to me that the real distinguishing characteristic of scientists is wonder. The decision to do science (or perhaps better, the orientation toward science) occurs early in life—perhaps having its origins in early childhood. All children are potentially scientists. Look at a child's eyes—they're wide with curiosity, wonder, and excitement, drinking in this lovely world. It's no accident that great artists and scientists alike have a childlike quality to them. I once said to a class that science is essentially "organized wonder," and that, when you're a small child the world is an incredibly exciting place in which everything calls to you, "Look at me! Look at me!" The sensory overload can be dizzying. Perhaps that's why young children sleep so soundly—they need time to process all that data. I remember when our children were very young, even though they were exhausted, we had to tell them to close their eyes so they could get to sleep. But it doesn't stop there. Those of us with children know that all this beauty and intricacy spawn an endless and often exasperating string of questions, all of which seem to involve the words "how" or "why."

Some people never get past that stage. They go through their lives with the bright eyes of children, endlessly interrogating the universe. It's not a habit they choose, but one, I suspect, that chooses them—a vocation, if you like. The best part of the whole business is that, if you never grow up, and you're very lucky, society lets you become a professional scientist; and they *pay* you for doing what you'd gladly do for nothing, which is a little like dying and going to heaven. A scientist has a unique opportunity as Robert Frost put it in his poem "Two Tramps in Mud Time," "to unite my vocation and my avocation, as my two eyes make one in sight." In the final analysis, then, a scientist is at root a lover, although this fact is often effectively hidden under an analytical facade.

This is, of course, not at all what most people think of when they think of science, which most people probably try to think of as little as possible. Ask virtually any person to describe science, and words like "exact" and "certain" will almost inevitably surface. The picture of a scientist in the popular imagination is of a dispassionate, objective observer, who stands apart from what he observes, and whose goal is to describe its composition, structure, and behavior exactly and completely. It is precisely this determination to understand reality *completely* that can seem to provide a major barrier between prayer and science—for nonscientists, because it seems to eliminate the sense of mystery and poetry in life, and for scientists because it makes them recoil from the prospect of grappling with an ultimately unknowable God. People don't like to set limits to either their God or their science.

But this inconsistency is only apparent because this idea of science became untenable in 1927 when Werner Heisenberg discovered the Uncertainty Principle, which probably ranks as one of *the* major philosophical principles of this century. Stephen Hawking, in his book *A Brief History of Time,* says that, a half-century after its discovery, the ramifications of this principle have not been fully appreciated, by either scientists or nonscientists.[1]

What is this principle of uncertainty, which has such a strange, unscientific-sounding name? Briefly, it says that you cannot determine exactly and simultaneously the position and momentum of a particle, no matter how hard you try, no matter how elaborate or sensitive your apparatus, no matter how subtle your experiment. The indeterminacy is not intellectual, or economic—it's a fundamental and inescapable feature of the world.

Now, what does this mean in English? Basically, that there are two types of questions we can pose to reality—one is essentially structural, because it deals with specifying position, and relative positions describe structure—and the other is essentially energetic. Heisenberg showed that there is a trade-off between the amounts of "positional" and "dynamic" information we can extract from a system—that the more precisely we try to define one, the less precisely we know the other. Imagine a pane of glass with the word "position" on the front face, and the word "momentum" on the back one. Put this in a slide projector and try to focus it. The more in focus the word "position" gets, the more out of focus the word "momentum" gets, and vice versa. We can choose to emphasize one or the other, but not both. In other words, the kinds of answers we get are conditioned by the kinds of questions we ask. Science and religion ask fundamentally different types of questions, so it's not surprising that they come away with fundamentally different types of answers. In that respect, I suppose my clerical friend is correct.

However, the fact that the answers are different doesn't mean that they have no relevance for each other, or that one must necessarily be true and the other false. In fact, in a while we'll encounter the so-called complementarity principle, discovered by the Danish physicist Niels Bohr, which says that what may appear to be opposite and incompatible descriptions are often found to be simultaneously true. Interestingly enough, when Heisenberg died in 1976, his friend and student Edward Teller, in an obituary in the journal *Nature*, wrote

> What are you: a piece of matter or a soul? It is difficult to deny either body or spirit. But to believe in both was considered sheer mysticism by a generation of scientists who lived in a world in which truth seemed to be simple . . . What has this [the Uncertainty Principle] to do with the body-spirit dualism? Heisenberg has shown that two obviously contradictory concepts, waves and

particles, are not only necessary in explaining the structure of atoms but also, these two concepts can coexist
within a single rigorous mathematical formalism. If this
can be done today for atoms why should it not be possible to do something similar someday in describing life
or even a human being?[2]

You can imagine the conflict this principle might engender in
the mind of a scientist, even a great one! Einstein, for one, found
the indeterminacy of wave mechanics very troubling, and went to
his grave convinced (or at least hoping!) that there was a flaw in
the reasoning. So far, though, no flaw has been found, and the
principle is now accepted as one of the centerpieces of contemporary physics.

I believe there's something here of direct relevance to the life of
prayer, and it can be summed up in a small sign my friends Peggy
and Tim have posted in the kitchen of their home in upstate New
York: "Prayer means getting hold of God, not the answer." Prayer
is, of course, communication with God, but too often we spend
time telling God all about ourselves, or demanding that God tell us
all about him/herself. The problem is that, as in science, there are
two types of questions we can ask: what God *is*—a structural (or
positional) question, and what God *does*—a dynamic question; and
the Uncertainty Principle suggests that the more we try to define
the one, the less we know about the other. This parallels my own
experience with prayer. For a long time, perhaps as a result of my
early religious and scientific training, I tried hard to understand
what God is, to make my prayer very intellectual. Not surprisingly, I came away with a static and rather constricted picture of
God. My experience was essentially lifeless, because, in trying to
define God, I was sacrificing a dynamic experience for a static one.
My prayer life really began to be transformed only when I stopped
trying to understand who God *is* and started paying attention to
what God *does*. God, in my experience, is in the transformation
business, so perhaps Peggy and Tim's sign really ought to read,
"Prayer means letting God get hold of us."

To help to illustrate what I mean, let me tell you a short story, a
parable, about my mother and her refrigerator. My mother is not a
scientist; she has never heard of the Joule-Thomson effect, and has
no idea how her refrigerator works. (Chances are most people

don't.) It's just a big tan box that stands in her kitchen, but it might as well be a *black* box, literally as well as figuratively. However, while she doesn't understand *how* it works, she understands and appreciates what it *does*: it keeps her food cold. I may not know exactly what God *is*, but that's all right, because I am learning what God *does* in my life, and I'll trade that dynamic information for the static stuff any day of the week.

There's another aspect of "seeing" I want to talk about. Beyond the *practice* of seeing—the habit of attentiveness—which comes naturally to scientists, lies the reality which is seen; and here I believe that scientists have a unique advantage—in breadth, certainly, but especially in depth. I mean that our training both enlarges and deepens our vision of the world, and this can immeasurably enrich our prayer life.

One of the ways in which being scientists enlarges our vision of the world is quantitatively. We're simply aware of a wider range of what I'll call conventionally beautiful natural phenomena, such as unusual animals, flowers, snowflakes, natural formations, crystals, molecules, sounds, and the like. Most scientists have a well-developed aesthetic sense, and since beauty makes a good starting point for prayer, a scientist who is also a believer does have an advantage. If you haven't watched crystal growth through a polarizing microscope, you've missed a lovely opportunity to praise God!

There can also be a *qualitative* advantage that comes from having a broader view of beauty. Unlike most nonscientists, scientists can find beauty in a well-planned chemical synthesis, in an elegant mathematical derivation, in a complex molecule, or in a biological process, as well as in sunsets, waterfalls and mountains; but it takes training and work, just as it does to appreciate the beauty in much of contemporary art and music. I've often been amazed to think of the intricacy and harmony of all the reactions that must occur simultaneously to maintain life, and it never fails to move me to prayer. Knowing more of the details than the average nonscientist doesn't detract from the beauty and mystery for me; it only *accentuates* it. The Nobel Prize-winning biochemist Albert Szent-Gyorgi said, in a somewhat different context, "Discovery consists in seeing what everyone else has seen and thinking what no one else has thought." Those discoveries make great starting points for prayer.

The science writer K. C. Cole, in her book of essays on physics, *Sympathetic Vibrations*, speaks of "seeing" as central to science. In a real sense, things don't exist for us until *someone* perceives them, or at least their effects. However, as the range and types and sensitivity of detectors increases, we become aware of more and more aspects, or types, of reality.

Cole points out that our "detectors" are sensitive to only a narrow range of signals:

> The pupil is but a tiny porthole in a sea of radiation. In a universe alight with images, we are mostly in the dark . . . I know that these signals are there, in the room with me, because if I flip on the radio or television I will suddenly be able to see or hear them—in the same ways that visions suddenly "appear" before me the minute I open my eyes. If I had still other kinds of detectors . . . I could pick up still other kinds of signals. Yet we walk through this dense web of radiant information every day without being in the least aware of its existence.[3]

For me that's a lot like prayer. I am surrounded by, bathed in, this tremendous reality named God, yet I am largely unaware of him, the only hint often being the wind of the Spirit blowing over what Peter Kreeft, in his book *Heaven, the Heart's Deepest Longing,* has called the "heaven-shaped hole in my heart."[4] My usual sensors aren't too good at detecting God, and the "signal" can sometimes be very weak, near the limit of detectability. I have a couple of choices available. First, of course, I can simply reject the data—define it away, call it an experimental aberration, a "glitch"—and close myself to a large part of reality. Or I can try to develop *new* sensors. I can refine my primary God-detector, my heart. Just as to hear a small sound I need to sit in silence and listen intently (increasing my signal-to-noise ratio by decreasing the interior noise), which allows me to become better able to detect variations, and nuances and subtleties, so in prayer I sit and listen, and you know, the more you listen, the more you hear.

Louis Pasteur said that "chance" favors the prepared mind. That's true. It's also true that God favors the prepared heart. The more intently and patiently and quietly you listen, the more the vibrations within you, the music of the spirit, intensify. It's amazing; the more you listen for God, the more you hear him!

Let's move away from principles for a moment to look at phenomena. One phenomenon in science which holds particular significance for me is resonance, because my research involves a branch of spectroscopy called Nuclear Magnetic Resonance, and also because I believe it can provide a different view of prayer.

To understand what resonance is, try an experiment next time you're in a shower stall or a telephone booth. Hum a note. (By the way, this works best if you're alone!) Chances are nothing much will happen at first. But, if you vary the pitch, at some point the enclosure will begin to vibrate in response. On a more familiar level, most people know that blowing over the mouth of an empty bottle will produce a musical note. Both of these responses occur because every system has one or more natural frequencies which correspond to the spacing between pairs of different energy states. If you supply an amount of energy that just matches one of those gaps, the system will absorb the energy and move from the lower to the next higher energy state. At that point it's said to be "excited." Spectroscopists use resonance to probe the energy gaps in systems by supplying electromagnetic radiation of different frequencies and watching for a response. A response indicates that the frequency of the radiation and the energy gap are exactly matched.

Prayer, for me, epitomizes resonance. It's a flow of energy. Not primarily from me to God, as we too often think of prayer, but from God to my soul. Peter Kreeft, as I mentioned earlier, has written that we're born with a heaven-shaped hole in our hearts, which nothing but God can fill. So often, as I quiet myself and sit in stillness, I experience a deep sense of peace, of what I can only describe as a feeling of "rightness," a conviction that I am where I'm supposed to be, and I know that this response, this resonance, is a sign that God's energy, God's grace, is flowing into my heart, filling it, and energizing me. What is energy, but the capacity to do work? What is grace, but God's capacity to work in me, changing me, building me up, transforming me into the image and likeness of my Lord?

In her book, *Sympathetic Vibrations*, K.C. Cole comments:

> It is no surprise to a physicist that a *thing* can be a "res-
> onant state," but it was certainly news to me. Little did
> I know that resonance was behind the very nature of
> matter—not to mention the sound of music, the color of
> autumn leaves, the rings of Saturn, the spectral lines
> that write the signatures of stars, and according to one
> source perhaps even the evolution of life. It accounts
> for everything from the low whistle of the wind over
> the Grand Canyon to the sound of a lover's voice.[5]

In prayer, we're responding to the sound of the voice of a loving God, and we become energized by grace. And, as if this
weren't enough, there's a bonus! Excited systems don't keep all
that new energy pent up inside of them, they spontaneously release it to their surroundings in a variety of ways, so that in addition to our becoming recipients of grace—the divine energy—that
energy flows out of us, and we become channels of grace for our
surroundings. We pass on the excitation.

Another principle that helps me to see how science can shed
light on prayer is the principle of complementarity. It seems to me
that complementarity really undermines the kind of smugness that
often seemed to characterize 19th century science. At the same
time, it echoes some familiar themes from major spiritual traditions, including Christianity.

What is complementarity? It arose out of the great scientific
controversy about the nature of light, which had been described
variously as either wavelike or particulate, with different ex-
periments supporting one or the other hypothesis. In 1924, the
French physicist Louis de Broglie proposed, on the basis of theoretical arguments, that matter can also behave as particle or wave,
depending on how it's interrogated—what type of experiment is
done. When this hypothesis was verified experimentally for elec-
trons by two Americans, Davisson and Germer, it became clear
that the *reality* exceeded our capacity to describe it, and scientists
were forced to the realization that even such apparently mutually
exclusive descriptions might be simultaneously correct. Not a case
of either/or, but of both/and.

It's important to recognize that our descriptions of reality—our theories—are both approximations and metaphors, and to keep always before our eyes their essential tentativeness, always to remember that the reality is always more complicated, or perhaps more *simple*, than we think. It's important to stand in awe before the *reality*, and not the *theory*. In the preface to his elementary text *Simple Inorganic Substances*, R. T. Sanderson puts it rather nicely.

> It seems to me that nature consists of an elaborate inter-commingling of marvelous simplicities with infinite complexities. I believe that the ultimate in truth and understanding is forever unattainable, but that human beings can deliberately create the illusion of understanding by recognizing and applying the simplicities in a useful way. We need not be embarrassed at the illusory nature of our understanding as long as it serves a useful purpose and we do not indulge in self-deception. More power to those who prefer to challenge their intellects by attempting to unravel the infinite complexities, but I think they should be careful neither to expect to win nor to convince themselves they have won.[6]

For a scientist to fall into Sanderson's trap of self-deception is, in effect, to lose touch with reality, and to enter into a kind of idolatry, to worship a graven image, rather than the creator.

Prayer, too, is a kind of exploration—a questing for the face of God. As in science, here too our limitations bump up against the immensity of God, who is far and away more complex—or perhaps better, more simple—than we can even *begin* to describe. We often wrestle with questions about how God can be both all-merciful and all-just; of how God, who claims to be always with us, can seem to be so absent from our lives; of how, if God has unlimited power, we have what appears to be a greater power—to frustrate or limit that power—the dilemma of God's limitedness. Like pre-twentieth century scientists we're all too often driven to insist on the truth of one or the other of these seemingly incompatible pairs, with the result that our attention shifts imperceptibly from God, who is ultimately beyond understanding or description, to our *picture* of God. This is rather like the self-centered person who monopolizes the conversation talking incessantly about himself, then stops and says "Well, enough about me; let's talk about you—how do you think I look?"

Even more than in science, in prayer it's important not to confuse the *illusion* of understanding with true understanding, to be humble in the face of both immensities—God, and the universe God created. A dozen years ago, when I first committed myself seriously to a relationship with God, I could have told you exactly what God was like and how God worked. In the intervening years, my experiences in the laboratory of prayer have been simultaneously enriching, frustrating, and humbling. If I had to write a laboratory report today, it would be short on facts, because most of my "certitudes" about God have melted away, but long on joy, because the only things I know for certain are that God *is* and that in his presence I am learning who *I* am.

What's happening in my prayer is that God is revealing me to me. On vacation in Maine a while ago, I was walking the beach, looking at the piles of seaweed that had washed up on the shore. Seaweed on the shore is thoroughly unappetizing-looking, brown and shriveled. But, when it's placed in water, something wonderful happens. It fans out into delicate and gentle, translucent leaves that move constantly and gracefully as the water stirs. Seaweed's element is not the air, it's water. Removed from it, it loses its beauty. Could anyone guess from seeing a pile of decaying, fly-infested, sun-blackened seaweed on the shore, what its true beauty and reality are? Maybe that's why Jesus said, "Anyone who does not live in me is like a withered, rejected branch, picked up to be thrown in the fire and burnt."[7] I'm learning, as time goes by, that *my* element is God's life. Without it, I'm dry and hard, nothing but fly food, food for the Lord of the Flies. But, immersed in it, I can unfold and become what I'm truly meant to be.

Science *can* seem threatening to people, and incompatible with faith, but, I think, only if it's seen in its pre-twentieth century, deterministic, arrogant incarnation. Take comfort, friends. For over sixty years that view has been insupportable, but the appropriation of that change by scientists and nonscientists alike requires three things: the awareness of these new (actually not-so-new) principles, the realization of their implications, and the willingness to let the old picture die a natural death. However, coping with death is no easier for scientists than for anyone else; we still go through the stages of denial, anger, bargaining, depression, and only at the last, acceptance.

Teilhard de Chardin wrote that science is the primary contemplative activity of our time, and this got me thinking about the contemplative aspect of science, and how that relates to the concept of extrapolation. Science has a dynamic character, and one of its driving forces is extrapolation. Our experience of reality is continuous, but data points are, of course, obtained individually and are often related to one another in graphical form. If the variation is smooth, the points can be connected by a continuous line. If the line is derived from a theoretical model, so much the better. As your eyes (and your mind) follow a line, the temptation to move beyond the points that define it—to extrapolate—becomes overwhelming. Waiting out there is unexplored territory—a chance to test your understanding against reality, with either emotional gratification, or crisis, lurking beyond each new experiment. While the gratification of a verified prediction is refreshing, it's not really filling, since all it really signals is that you haven't reached the frontiers of your understanding. Total disagreement with expectation is far better in the long run, because it precipitates a crisis which forces a complete reappraisal of your ideas. Someone told me that the Chinese character for "crisis" contains two parts: one meaning "danger," the other meaning "opportunity." I have an acquaintance at Harvard Medical School who, when research students tell him they've run into a problem, always answers aggressively, "You don't have a problem, you have an opportunity!" The basic idea is that beyond what we understand, there is always more to know. I remember vividly last summer a visiting priest in our parish preaching about the inexhaustibility of the experience of God, stalking up and down the aisle, insisting "The more! Always the more!"

As it is in science, so it is in life. While the basic data never change, the hypotheses that give them meaning change, enlarging our vision, so that their significance becomes greater and their connection to other data becomes broadened, in the limit, encompassing a single, undivided reality which we, because of our finite minds, need to compartmentalize.

Not too long ago I was at Mass, and the gospel reading of the day dealt with John the Baptist's identification of Jesus as the Messiah. My mind keeps coming back to the verse where John the Baptist says of Jesus, "I confess I did not recognize him, though the very reason I came baptizing with water was that he might be revealed to Israel."[8] Something in John (a fire in the heart) called him out into the desert to think, to contemplate, and then drove him back out of the desert with a message to proclaim—but what message? A partial one at best, the discovery of which enriched both others and himself. Almost certainly the truth of his "discovery" far outstripped what he knew or could even begin to understand. But that didn't stop him from proclaiming it. The key is less to understand fully than to hand on what you've discovered—to project (extrapolate) it into the future in an act of faith and hope. Someone—I can't recall who—observed that unless it's possible to understand something without understanding everything, then it's impossible ever to understand anything, or to put it more scripturally, we can say, with St. Paul, "Now we see indistinctly, as in a mirror; then we shall see face to face. My knowledge is imperfect now; then I shall know even as I am known."[9]

Thomas Merton, in his poem "The Quickening of St. John the Baptist," speaks of the monastic vocation in words that could equally well be applied to the scientist:

> Night is our diocese and silence is our ministry
> Poverty our charity and helplessness our tongue-tied sermon.
> Beyond the scope of sight or sound we dwell upon the air
> Seeking the world's gain in an unthinkable experience.
> We are exiles in the far end of solitude, living as listeners
> With hearts attending to the skies we cannot understand:
> Waiting upon the first far drums of Christ the Conqueror,
> Planted like sentinels upon the world's frontier.[10]

Creation is a solitary, meditative, often frustrating, process with the most intense work being done at the subconscious level. The glimmering of an idea may linger in half-light, rolling around near the tip of your tongue, but seem never to be ready to move, fully-formed, out into the light of day. But all of us who have done creative work know that when it comes, it brings an indescribably intense feeling of elation! Merton continues,

> Cooled in the flame of God's dark fire,
> Washed in His gladness like a vesture of new flame
> We burn like eagles in his invincible awareness
> And bound and bounce with happiness,
> Leap in the womb, our cloud, our faith, our element,
> Our contemplation, our anticipated Heaven
> Til Mother Church sings like an Evangelist.

As scientists, we're also waiting for the revelation of the truth, although we would not all (at least consciously!) mean the same thing by it, and would almost certainly not characterize it in Merton's words! But the form of expression is far less important than the fact that we are waiting and longing for this revelation, this knowledge, for what is this but the action of a lover?

For a moment, think about falling in love. First you glimpse someone far off and are intrigued—not by true understanding, but on a purely physical level—the color of her hair, or the grace of her stature, or her shape, by the way she's put together. This isn't really love, just fascination, because at this point she's just an *object*, but it can be the first step on the path that leads to love.

As you move in closer, the knowledge becomes more personal—you invest yourself in it—interaction occurs, and you begin to see beyond the surface, to the reality beyond appearance. It becomes part of you and you a part of it. *This* is where love begins.

What is the love that science can bring us to? It's seeing the unity of creation—the face of God reflected in the faces of his creatures, and this brings me to the concept of feedback, on which a true love-relationship is built, and which is, for me, the glue that unites my life of science and my life of prayer.

For almost twenty-five years now I've walked through the front entrance of Devlin Hall nearly every day, mostly oblivious to the verse from Paul's letter to the Romans inscribed above it. Paul wrote: "Since the creation of the world, invisible realities, God's eternal power and divinity, have become visible, recognized through the things he has made."[11] This, it seems to me, is essentially the vision of St. Ignatius—that we're never closer to God than when we're engaged with the world, through which God is revealed, that when as scientists we confront the universe, we're on holy ground, and we should study it on our knees. Viewed in this light, studying science shouldn't move us *away* from God, but *toward* him. In his marvelous book *For the Life of the World,* the Orthodox theologian Alexander Schmemann writes of Christ:

> As Christians we believe that He, who is the truth about both God and man, gives foretastes of His incarnation in all more fragmentary truths. We believe as well that Christ is present in any seeker after truth. Simone Weil has said that though a person may run as fast as he can away from Christ, if it is toward what he considers true, he runs in fact into the arms of Christ.[12]

For a scientist who also has the good fortune to be a believer, a kind of cycle develops: authentic love of God doesn't draw us away from the world, but sends us back into it with recreated vision, by which we encounter God in all his works. This, in turn, sends us to the Father with a song of praise in our hearts. Who said "and every bush is aflame with God?" Psalms 19 and 29, or the words of one of my favorite hymns, "How Great Thou Art," are good illustrations of this. And we cycle back and forth in a kind of upward-spiraling feedback loop, until our lives become truly integrated, when God permeates every moment, when we're in constant communion with him, as Jesus was, as St. Francis was. In reading the saints—like Teresa of Avila, or Francis of Assisi, or Thomas Merton—I'm constantly struck by their lack of "other-worldliness," by their intense awareness of, and involvement with, and interest in, the mundane details of life—Merton's photographs of the most ordinary objects, for example. I used to find them a bit confusing—often not beautiful aesthetically—and boring; but now I'm beginning to appreciate the childlike simplicity that delights in God's creation, and for which (as Michel Quoist says in his book, *Prayers,* many of whose meditations are based on the very ordinary) "all of life would become a sign."[13]

The last aspect of science I'd like to look at is the growing sense of the interdependence of all of creation, and I want to give examples from two widely divergent branches of science, biology and physics. There are two general approaches in science, the analytical and the synthetic. In the early stages of any science, the only reasonable way to proceed is analytically—to select what you want to study, and to examine it as an individual, in isolation from its surroundings. Now, while this is a useful way to characterize individual objects, organisms, or phenomena, it's not effective for studying systems or processes, which are based on interrelations among individuals. That's why as sciences mature, their approach becomes increasingly synthetic. It becomes clear that the sense of individuality is largely a convenient fiction. This theme permeates the writings of the eminent physician and essayist Lewis Thomas. In a Phi Beta Kappa address he delivered at Harvard, entitled "The Uncertainty of Science," Thomas said,

> One major question needing to be examined is the general *attitude* of nature. A century ago there was a consensus about this: nature was "red in tooth and claw," evolution was a record of open warfare among competing species, the fittest were the strongest aggressors, and so forth. Now it begins to look different. The tiniest and most fragile organisms dominate the life of the earth: the chloroplasts inside the cells of plants, which turn solar energy into food and supply the oxygen for breathing, appear to be the descendants of ancient blue-green algae, living now as permanent lodgers within the cells of "higher" forms; the mitochondria of all nucleated cells, which serve as engines for all the functions of life, are the progeny of bacteria which took to living as cells inside cells long ago. The urge to form partnerships, to link up in collaborative arrangements, is perhaps the oldest, strongest and most fundamental force in nature. There are no solitary, free-living creatures; every form of life is dependent on other forms. The great successes in evolution, the mutants who have, so to speak, made it, have done so by fitting in with, and sustaining, the rest of life. Up to now, we might be counted among the brilliant successes, but flashy and perhaps unstable. We should go warily into the future, looking for ways to be more useful, listening more carefully for the signals, watching our step, and having an eye out for partners.[14]

Does this have a familiar ring? Among living things, on both the physical and spiritual levels, the operative principle is symbiosis. We can only express truly who we are, in relationship.

A similar picture comes from physics. Almost everyone would identify gravity as the force by which two objects are attracted to each other. However, the theory of relativity, developed by Einstein in the early decades of this century, considers gravity to be, not a force, but a property of space. If space were flat, an object in motion would move in a perfectly straight line. However, any object curves the space around it, like a dimple in a sheet of rubber. Consequently, when another moves by it, it is diverted from its straight path and the two objects appear to be attracted to each other. Thus, the properties of space, and therefore the behavior of every object in the universe, is influenced by every other object, even the most seemingly insignificant one. The physicist Michael Berry said this about the effect of the smallest perturbation imaginable—a single electron at the edge of the universe:

> A single electron. Just one. There it is at the observable limit of the universe, say ten thousand million light years away. It has its gravitational effect, but you don't know where it is exactly, so that's the uncertainty. Well, you ask, after how many collisions will the little uncertainty that's produced in a motion by that electron be amplified to the degree where you've lost all predictability . . . Well, the amazing thing is that the number of collisions is only about 50 or so, which is of course over in a tiny, tiny fraction of a microsecond.[15]

No one is unimportant. One life, one act, one word, has the capacity to change the world.

As I reflect on these examples, I can't help but recall St. Paul's image of the body of Christ, with each person contributing to the creation and functioning of a reality which transcends all of us, with all of life linked in a web of relationships, and I feel comforted that the wisdom of science and the wisdom of God are perhaps not so far apart after all.

In a way, this brings us back to where we began, with science as "organized wonder." If we enter into it, this wonder gives rise to a song in our hearts. Filled with joy, the true scientist hears the music and is drawn to a kind of "worship," but at this stage it's an incomplete worship, a worship of a nameless God, a situation similar to that of the Athenians to whom St. Paul was speaking when he said:

> As I walked through your city and looked at the places where you worship, I found also an altar on which is written, 'To an unknown God.' That which you worship, then, even though you do not know it, is what I now proclaim to you. God, who made the world and everything in it, is Lord of heaven and earth, and does not live in [human] temples. Nor does God need anything that [anyone] can supply by working for him, since it is God himself who gives life and breath and everything else to [everyone]. . . . God did this so that they would look for him, and perhaps find him as they felt around for him. Yet God is actually not far from any one of us; as someone has said, "In him we live, and move, and have our being."[16]

The crucial difference for the believer is the intervention of faith. Faith supplies the vision—the words to the music, completing the song—a symbiosis, each part completing and giving meaning to the other in a rising spiral. Remember the man in the 9th chapter of John's gospel whom Jesus cured of blindness. He rejoiced in his vision, without knowing who it was who cured him. But, his joy was completed when he learned who it was who cured him.

I've tried to share with you some of the connections I've made on my own continuing spiritual journey. I claim no special authority or profundity for them, but they've gladdened my heart and enriched my life, and perhaps they'll help to enrich yours. They may not, but in the final analysis, that's not particularly important. It's not *my* job to transform your life, or even my own life—it's God's, and I *know* it's happening right now. My job is simply to be true to my triple vocation as scientist, teacher, and Christian, by seeking the truth, by honoring it when I encounter it, and by handing it on. You have a similar calling.

We are *all* searchers, and what each of us is ultimately seeking is the revelation of our true self. Only God can reveal that secret to us, and the place where that work will be accomplished is the laboratory of prayer, where Jesus will remake us into new creations, with new eyes, and renewed minds, and recreated hearts, and the one thing about which I have absolutely no doubt is that it will happen. I'd like to close by recalling the reassuring words of St. Paul who, looking down the centuries, was surely thinking of all of us when he said,

> To him who is able to do immeasurably more than all we ask or imagine, according to his power that is at work within us, to him be glory in the church and in Christ Jesus, throughout all generations, for ever and ever. Amen.[17]

9

Prayer and Work

Richard Carroll Keeley

To help us to meditate on the theme of "prayer and work" I ask my readers to try to imagine with me a stained-glass triptych. The triptych I am imagining is one of the windows in the beautiful chapel dedicated to Mary at St. Mary's Hall, the Jesuit residence at Boston College. Its theme fits our topic perfectly.

In the left panel, Elizabeth and the young John the Baptist—he clothed, precociously, in his garment of camel-hair—turn towards the middle panel where a radiant Jesus and his mother, Mary, stand upon the threshold. In the right panel, Joseph sits. He wears a carpenter's smock but, at this moment, he does not answer the call of his trade. A hatchet lies at his feet; behind him, a hammer lies untouched upon a table; a saw dangles from his left hand, its tip resting lightly against the ground. His right hand supports his head and we regard Joseph caught in a moment of contemplation: his eyes have a deep focus, their object unknown. Perhaps he thinks, we might muse, of his absent family or the extraordinary circumstances of their life together: these would be fitting thoughts for a workman on his break, the stuff of everyday reverie at the workplace. But as our eyes mount to the top of the triptych, we realize that no such thoughts distract Joseph at this moment: he is at prayer, his work laid aside. For atop the left and right panels, joining and crowning the scene, two angels unfurl banners: "Ora et" reads the inscription on the left, "labora" answers the inscription on the right, "pray and work."

That simple phrase captures much, not all, of the Christian tradition's concern with prayer and work. Note, first, the sequence: prayer takes priority. Note also, though, that both are commended; we are not offered an exclusive choice. Note, finally, the suggestion, embodied in the artifice of the separate panels themselves, that prayer and work belong in separate categories. Joseph must lay aside his tools and his worldly concerns in order to pray. (We recall, on this score, the story of Martha and Mary: the busy Martha, resentful of Mary's putting aside the household tasks to enjoy the company of Jesus, learns from Jesus himself to 'put first things first.' Between work and prayer, we might infer, the choice is always clear.)

The window may carry a subtler message as well. It may suggest a definition of prayer, a definition with deep roots in traditional Catholic formation. In prayer, I learned from catechism, I lift the mind and heart to God. Mind and heart are, in the moment of prayer, directed to their true origin and destiny. That redirection, however, depends upon a certain discipline and may require a special place. I must surmount my ordinary concerns to elevate mind and heart; I must, with Joseph, lay aside the tools of my trade. A prayer not so disciplined might become a self-absorbed interior monologue, rather than a God-seeking dialogue.

Still, if we conceive of prayer in this way, we might sense that the seeming balance of the banners' message—pray *and* work—is quite seriously out of kilter. Prayer begins where work leaves off, for work impedes prayer by occupying mind and heart, to say nothing of body. If you would pray, we might conclude, cease to work.

At this point I should note an irony in the placement of this window above an altar dedicated to Ignatius. It consists in this: the phrase "Pray and work" better represents St. Benedict's theology, not that of St. Ignatius. In writing his Rule for monastic life, Benedict enjoined the monks to daily manual labor since "idleness is an enemy of the soul. Therefore," he continues, "the brothers should be occupied according to schedule in either manual labor or holy reading."[1] Work, on this understanding, is good insofar as it occupies the soul, which otherwise might be led astray by the thoughts idleness fosters. What is lacking, on the face of it, in Benedict's formulation, is any appreciation of the intrinsic goodness of work, let alone its possible prayerfulness. Might there be something prayerful in work itself? Could the heart and mind and body *engaged* in work be lifted up to God?

I want to approach these questions indirectly, via a story. The story is Raymond Carver's "A Small, Good Thing."[2] Those of you who know this piece will understand why I recommend it with a special warning to parents: it is the story of the accidental death of a young boy, an only child, and I, at least, cannot read it without tears.

The outlines of the plot, as in most Carver stories, are easily limned. A mother orders a special birthday cake for her son, Scotty, from a taciturn baker who refuses all of her friendly overtures. "The baker, who was an older man with a thick neck, listened without saying anything. . . . He wiped his hands on his apron as he listened to her. He kept his eyes down on the photographs and let her talk. He let her take her time. He'd just come to work and he'd be there all night, baking, and he was in no real hurry. . . . There were no pleasantries between them, just the minimum exchange of words, the necessary information. . . . She. . . . wondered if he'd ever done anything else with his life besides be a baker. . . . She gave up trying to make friends with him."[3] While walking home from school on his birthday, the boy is struck by a car and eventually lapses into a coma. Father and mother hold bedside vigil. On quick, solitary trips home to bathe or feed the dog, they are interrupted by a series of brusque phone calls—the reader immediately recognizes the caller—inquiring about Scotty and what they have forgotten. The cake has gone unclaimed and unpaid for and the baker, ignorant of the developing tragedy, exacts revenge by calling, anonymously, at all hours of the day and night. After the boy has died and both parents are home, he calls once more and this time, the mother knows: it is the baker and now she wants revenge. In the early morning hours, they drive to the bakery and confront the baker in his kitchen.

One might expect an abrupt end to the story at this point, a termination in confrontation and recrimination, but Carver surprises us, for after a brief outburst of righteous anger from the mother, here is what happens. "The baker had cleared a space for them at the table. He shoved the adding machine to one side, along with the stacks of notepaper and receipts. He pushed the telephone directory onto the floor, where it landed with a thud. Howard and Ann sat down and pulled their chairs up to the table. The baker sat down, too."[4] Having cleared a space for them to gather, the baker begins an apology, a confession and concludes with a plea for forgiveness. "Let me say how sorry I am. . . . God alone knows how sorry. Listen to me. I'm just a baker. I don't claim to be anything else. Maybe once, maybe years ago, I was a different kind of human being. I've forgotten, I don't know for sure. But I'm not any longer, if I ever was. Now I'm just a baker. That don't excuse my doing what I did, I know. . . . You got to understand what it comes down to is I don't know how to act anymore, it would seem. Please," the man said, "let me ask if you can find it in your hearts to forgive me?"[5]

Silence enfolds the parents and in the silence, the baker sets the table with coffee, cream and sugar. "'You probably need to eat something,' the baker said.' I hope you'll eat some of my hot rolls. You have to eat and keep going. Eating is a small, good thing in a time like this,' he said. . . . 'It's good to eat something,' he said, watching them. 'There's more. Eat up. Eat all you want. There's all the rolls in the world in here.'"[6]

And after eating, talk begins. It is the baker speaking but Carver suppresses the actual voice and presents this resumé:

> Then he began to talk. They listened carefully. Although they were tired and in anguish, they listened to what the baker had to say. They nodded when the baker began to speak of loneliness, and of the sense of doubt and limitation that had come to him in his middle years. He told them what it was like to be childless all these years. To repeat the days with the ovens endlessly full and endlessly empty. . . . He had a necessary trade. He was a baker. He was glad he wasn't a florist. It was better to be feeding people. This was a better smell anytime than flowers.[7]

Carver then allows the baker's voice to be heard one final time:

"Smell this," the baker said, breaking open a dark loaf. "It's a heavy bread, but rich." They smelled it, then he had them taste it. It had the taste of molasses and coarse grains. They listened to him. They ate what they could. They swallowed the dark bread. It was like daylight under the fluorescent trays of light. They talked on into the early morning, the high, pale cast of light in the windows, and they did not think of leaving.[8]

To return to our questions: might there be something prayerful in work itself? Could the mind, heart and body engaged in work be lifted up to God? Yes, asserts this story, this might be possible. "A Small, Good Thing" exemplifies what I call the 'Eucharistic' dimension of work, work as a giving of thanks and a forgiving reception of oneself. At the same time, it demonstrates how work may be profaned by becoming a means of isolation, an effort directed towards the interest of a solitary self.

At the beginning of the story, Carver presents the baker as a solitary person who spurns the human touch. He listens without responding, keeps his eyes down, refuses to allow friendliness to enter into a commercial transaction. A job is a job is a job, his attitude seems to say. He has, as he admits at story's end, forgotten how to be with other people, so encased has he become in the daily round of orders, proofing the yeast, tending the ovens. But he is not alone in this failing, even if he represents an extreme case. There's a description of the boy's father, Howard, on route from the hospital to home, thinking: "Until now, his life had gone smoothly and to his satisfaction—college, marriage, another year of college for the advanced degree in business, a junior partnership in an investment firm. Fatherhood. He was happy and, so far, lucky—he knew that. . . . So far, he had kept away from any real harm, from those forces he knew existed and that could cripple or bring down a man if the luck went bad, if things suddenly turned."[9] For Howard, work forms part of a grand strategy for a purchase on seeming invulnerability: work, and other things, distract him from the ordinary and special terrors of life (and from its ordinary and special joys, as well, we might suspect). With his luck run out, he sees the strategy for what it is, a self-imposed and failed ruse. Only Doctor Franklin, the child's physician, seems able to integrate work and vulnerability, professional skill and the human touch. When he comforts Anne after Scotty's death, Carver tells us, "Dr. Francis was shaken." He does not deny loss or minimize pain. "At one point, he leaned over and embraced her. She could feel his chest rising and falling evenly against her shoulder."[10] To Ann "he seemed full of some goodness she did not understand."[11]

At the story's end, this 'goodness' reappears in the baker's act, this time not a 'fullness' but 'a small, good thing,' the offer of food and drink. The first food is sweet and the hungry people consume the rolls quickly. Later, the baker offers more substantial fare, 'a dark loaf, . . . heavy bread but rich' and 'they ate what they could.' In the breaking of both kinds of bread there is recognition—of the parents as parents in their grief, of the baker as lonely in his isolation—fellowship, conversation, forgiveness. There is, in short, an epiphany of eucharist. Differences are overcome, anger put aside, three people are joined as one in deep conversation, nourished by the food and by each other and 'they did not think of leaving.' Work, which had seemed a cycle of 'days with the ovens endlessly full and endlessly empty,' the days of which the Preacher in Ecclesiastes complains, has become transformed. The baker's work has brought people together, fed them, given them an occasion to find a common language with which to speak of, and know, themselves and others. The 'small, good thing' of eating prepares them for the greater, daunting tasks of human life together.

Does what I have said thus far amount to dissolving the distinction between work and prayer or suggesting that work always reveals a eucharistic dimension? By no means. The story we have been considering suggests quite the contrary.

In speaking of work's Eucharistic dimensions, I'm describing possibilities, not asserting certainties. Work can be little more than a means of passing time to secure the basic necessities of life or the instrument for getting the luxury, power and status that lifts one above the realm of necessity; both those options are pursued in the story we have just considered. But there are depths and fullness, good things small and great, to be discovered within, and just below, the contours of ordinary work. In speaking of work as eucharist, I invite you to think about work as a sacrament, a special means of grace. And I would like you to join with me now in thinking about the special characteristics of the sacrament of the Eucharist.

It is a meal but not the ordinary fare we expect in a fast food culture. For one thing, it satisfies real hungers, a hunger for God and a hunger for fellowship with our brothers and sisters. This needs more comment: eucharist is not a meal to be taken alone, spiritual food snatched on the sly. At its heart lies communion, table fellowship: homilists often, rightly, talk about it as a 'family reunion.' If we probe the reunion image, we see that it captures something of the structure and rhythm of the liturgy.

As a family reunion, Eucharist promotes the sharing of memories: it recollects our history. We begin the eucharistic celebration with a recollection of who we are and how we have failed and we ask forgiveness. We meditate upon the story of the one, Jesus, who has made us his brothers and sisters, all God's children, and we listen, as well, to the prophets who preceded him and the witnesses who followed him in the early church. Forgiven and instructed, we stand to confess our faith and place ourselves in prayer before God. The rhythm of recollection returns as the celebrant prepares for, then prays, the consecration. Indeed, the technical term for this prayer is the *anamnesis*, or recollection. We recall that on the night before he died, Jesus gathered his friends at table, took bread, blessed and broke it, blessed wine as well and proclaimed them His Body and Blood, offered on our behalf. We recall, too, the final promise that he would be with us whenever we so gathered and remembered. As we continue with the celebration, memory stirs again: our community is one of the living and the dead, we pray with and for them. And, shortly later, we are joined with them, mystically, as we approach the table of the Lord.

All that recollection with all of those friends, present or departed, gives us a name, a place, a vocation. Indeed, Eucharist concludes with commissioning: go forth to love and serve the Lord. And for that, and all that precedes it, we say, "Thanks be to God."

Now, how might work be eucharist for us? Allow me to focus on the verbs I used to describe what happens to us, and what we do, in the celebration of Eucharist. Eucharist *gathers* a community, eucharist *recollects* the history of that community, eucharist *extends and deepens* our identity in that recollected gathering, eucharist *transforms* bread and wine into Jesus, broken for us, and our hopes, fears, failings and achievements into the stuff of prayer, eucharist *sustains and invigorates*. I think that work shares many of these possibilities.

Work *gathers* a community. People come together about a common task. Oftentimes, that cooperation is immediately visible and tangible: the office environment, the machine-shop floor. At other times, it's invisible but nevertheless real: the research scientist in Chestnut Hill knows his community extends to New York and Palo Alto, Berlin and Tokyo. In and through work, people create common ground. The product is the most easily appreciated commonality but no less real or important is the potential to enjoy the company of others.

Work *recollects* the community. All work, even work characterized as "at the cutting edge" or "on the frontiers of knowledge," depends on old work. While teaching appears a solitary undertaking, it presupposes the teacher's teachers and how they formed him, as well as the school's founders and the sacrifices they made to preserve the institution. The piece of finished chrome which ornaments a car carries the labor of many hands and processes. The word processing program hides years of work in mathematics and circuit design as well as assembly and production. Work, in short, can tell us much about who we are—and whom we owe. We are creatures who make things—by hand, by thought, by machine—sometimes alone but more often with others and always against a backdrop which we did *not* create but without which we could not be who we are.

Work *extends and deepens* our identity. Good work challenges us to grow in skill and wisdom. We have all had the experience of how problems at work absorb our attention and the exhilaration which greets their solution. We feel happy, satisfied, fuller. We spend ourselves in work and every extension of the self builds a capacity for greater development. Failures have a special importance here: they are, potentially, seed-ground for wisdom. When I bump up against my misunderstanding or lack of competence, my limitations, I have the opportunity to grow in wisdom and self-acceptance.

Work *transforms*. At its most basic level, work involves the transformation of material: a tree becomes lumber becomes boards and paper and so forth, through the transforming activity of the human being. If we raise our sights another notch, we appreciate work as a way of transforming the world entrusted to us by God. Our work can seek to build a fitting city for all of humankind, an anticipation of the Kingdom. We are ourselves transformed in work, brought out of isolation and called to cooperate, challenged to develop skills and to provide for family and the larger community.

Finally, work *sustains and invigorates*. The products of our work form the basis for maintaining human life. Work is a continuing process of exchange: I give myself over to some task and my giving over both reshapes me and realizes something new. And in some sense, this giving over of myself is a thanks-giving, an acknowledgment of my need to enter into exchange with the world. Simone Weil is especially suggestive on this point: "The world only gives itself to Man in the form of food and warmth if Man gives himself to the world in the form of labor."[12]

And so, I suggest that work is a kind of Eucharist. It is a way to knowing myself and my ties to others, it satisfies my desire to be of use, it contributes to the building up of the human community even as it shapes and perfects my abilities.

Each of us ought to review our work in these Eucharistic terms. Let me also suggest some other ways of thinking about the prayerfulness of work.

In the Genesis creation account, the human being is described as made in the image of God. The serpent tempts Adam and Eve with this in mind, perhaps: You shall be like God! One way of understanding sin, I think, is forgetting that we are the images of God and fancying ourselves our own god, our own trinity of creator, redeemer, sanctifier. But if we can appreciate ourselves as images of God, we may be able to see some resemblance between our work and God's.

While we do not create *ex nihilo*, we might identify some aspects of work as "creative." The natural law tradition, of which E. F. Schumacher is a good, popular representative, saw in work an opportunity for the individual to draw into communion with others, to enlarge his understanding and perfect his talents, to serve the purposes of the human community.[13] Such work was "good" and I think we can see a correspondence between work so described and the mighty act of God in Genesis: chaos gives way to order, the universe teems with life and God's irrepressible love issues in human community. Where our work serves to unite, instruct, perfect and sustain the human project, we are co-operators with God in creation.

Work may *redeem* as well as create. When I say "redeem" I do not mean to suggest that we save ourselves: that redemption is the work of God in Christ. But I do want to suggest that our work has a redemptive quality in the unfolding of God's purposes. It may help to begin with some word-play here: listen to these definitions of "redeem" drawn from the Oxford American Dictionary. "To buy back, to recover (a thing) by payment or by doing something. . . . to clear a debt. . . . to purchase the freedom (of a person) by payment. . . . to save from damnation or the consequences of sin. . . . to make up for faults and deficiencies." Now all of these definitions, with the exception of the next to last, to save from damnation or the consequences of sin, can be understood in simple, secular terms. We submit coupons or ransom hostages or pay off mortgages, all in the name of "redemption." But we can experiment and use these definitions as metaphors for considering the prayerfulness of work from another dimension.

"To buy back, to recover a thing by payment or by doing something:" these phrases suggest work which involves recovery of what is lost, repair and restoration of what has been damaged, replenishment of what has been depleted. In turn, recovery, repair, restoration and replenishment point to a spirituality of work as stewardship, a careful marshalling, use and preservation of what has been given to us. A wide range of people qualify as stewards: the garbagemen and sanitation workers who keep streets clean and healthy; the crews which repair roads and keep communication equipment on line; the city manager who dedicates herself to the preservation of good order and a flourishing life in her community.

"To clear a debt." The great French political theorist Montesquieu wrote that "At our coming into the world, we contract an immense debt to our country, which we can never discharge." He was thinking of all that we take for granted: the gifts which are our heritage of language, custom, law, family, religion, all of which predate our birth and indicate the general lines of our yet-to-be-developed humanity. Though we Americans prize fiercely our individualism, we are, unwittingly, the recipients of an immense collective gift, our culture (in the broadest sense). The work which best corresponds to clearing a debt, in this sense of redemption, is teaching. The teacher, and here I include parents, introduces the student to the mystery of the world, gives a primary orientation to its contours. I am thinking of education as something more than the transmission of facts and information: equally important is the stimulation of wonder, a tutelage in the rigors of thought, a cultivation of a sense of beauty and the moral imagination.

"To purchase the freedom of a person." Who lacks freedom in our society? They are legion: the addicted, the illiterate, the hopeless, the homeless, the unreflective consumer, those convicted of crime, and these are but a few. How might their freedom be purchased? We have a common, Christian obligation to purchase the freedom of those imprisoned around us. But my description of kinds of unfreedom points to specific kinds of work which redeem by helping to 'purchase' freedom. I think of the counsellors of the addicted, the teachers of literacy, the staff of shelters for the homeless, mental health workers.

"To make up for faults and deficiencies." Redemptive work corrects. Such is the work of the physical therapist, criminal justice officials, social workers and doctors. Notice that this kind of work usually involves engagement with a history of suffering, loss, abuse or deprivation. It strives to compensate, to make-up; only rarely will it fully restore. But those engaged in these works have, perhaps, an unusual opportunity for responding to the call to love one's neighbor.

To complete our trinitarian reflection, we need to ask how work may sustain and sanctify, or make holy, human life. Here, I find that I need to change my direction somewhat. When I spoke about work as creative or redemptive, I began by seeking analogies between our undertakings and the missions of God the Father and Jesus, looking for potentially salvific dimensions of our work. When we examined opportunities to create or redeem, we then asked how they might share in, or at least reflect, God's continuing creative and redemptive work. Here's my change: I want to begin by asking, more specifically than I have before, about the mission of the Holy Spirit. No full-blown theology, here, just a consideration of several Pauline texts.

In the Letter to the Romans, Paul tells us "The Spirit too comes to help us in our weakness. For when we cannot find words to pray, the Spirit himself expresses our plea in a way that could never be put into words, and God who knows everything in our hearts knows perfectly well what he means. . . ." In First Corinthians, he describes the Spirit as conferring a variety of gifts, each different but each conducing to the spiritual welfare of the community. And in Galatians, he enumerates the fruits of the Spirit's gifts: "love, joy, peace, patience, kindness, goodness, trustfulness, gentleness and self-control." These three passages show the Holy Spirit to be so intimate with us, and with God, that it is difficult to determine where—or whether—we leave off and the Spirit begins.

And that's my point: the sanctification of the world proceeds by the power of the Spirit in us as we carry it forth. If you ask, "How does work sanctify?," I respond, "Look for instances where work issues in love, joy, peace, patience, kindness, goodness, trustfulness, gentleness and self-control. Do you know families where those qualities shine? There, life is sanctified, holy. Do you know offices and workplaces where those gifts reign? There, work sanctifies, makes holy."

Let me suggest, finally, that we consult an aspect of our tradition which has suffered a partial eclipse. I am referring to the corporal and the spiritual works of mercy. The corporal works of mercy, adumbrated in Matthew 25:31-46, are: to feed the hungry, to give drink to the thirsty, to clothe the naked, to visit the imprisoned, to shelter the homeless, and to bury the dead. The spiritual works of mercy are: to admonish the sinner, to instruct the ignorant, to counsel the doubtful, to comfort the sorrowful, to bear wrongs patiently, to forgive all injuries and to pray for the living and the dead.[14] We can ask about the points of convergence, both literal and figurative, between our work and these works.

I think we may be surprised at the number of times they intersect. Return to that meeting in the early morning hours in a bakery between a baker and two sorrowing parents where shelter is given, food provided, forgiveness extended and the prison of lone-liness gives way to community. Small moments, good moments, moments such as we may encounter every day when we may work and pray.

10

Praying Through the Non-Christian

Francis X. Clooney, S.J.

I

During 1982-83 I lived in Madras, India, doing research in classical Hindu texts. Aiming toward the completion of my graduate studies, I was engaged in a planned, well-plotted academic journey through the technical territory of a great non-Western theological tradition. Despite the heat and the mosquitoes, I learned a great deal about Hindu thought, ancient and modern, was able to complete my studies as planned, and even modified the way I think theologically. But as is often the case, more than planned took place, for my time in Madras included a number of unexpected moments and encounters, small events which changed my thinking and praying in important ways. One of these occurred when I visited Tirupati.

Tirupati, a few hours by bus north of Madras into the state of Andhra Pradesh, is the site of a famous temple more than 1500 years old, dedicated to the Hindu deity Visnu who, in a variety of forms, is one of the most important deities of India today. Tirupati is a very popular, well-maintained and well-endowed temple; high on a hill and blessed with a refreshing waterfall, it is also a lovely and attractive respite from the dry and hot plains below.

When I visited there, I had the good fortune to be accompanied by a young professor of Sanskrit from Madras, whose acquaintance with a temple priest gave us a place to stay overnight, and gave me an entrée into the temple life beyond that ordinarily available to the foreign tourist. Our host awakened us at 3 A.M. and invited us to come to the "waking up" ceremony at the inner sanctum of the temple, just beneath its gleaming golden dome. We joined a few devotees there, who were chanting morning hymns in honor of Visnu. Then, the door to the inner sanctum was opened and the devotees removed the ceremonial bedding, and other articles that had been left near the most holy, central image of Visnu during the night; finally, they brought in food and water for the ceremonial and symbolic morning sacraments of purification which are performed before the image.

We then joined the devotees in entering the sanctum one by one, to pass down the narrow passageway that leads to the central image. We were allowed to spend a few moments there before returning by the passageway on the other side. Dark, lit only by small oil lamps, scented with incense and fresh flowers, gleaming gold and silver, the passageway led me to a sacred image which was iconographically so different from the Christian, so differently evocative. Yet I was entering an environment rich in piety and, I learned, into the transcendent, the holy. To stand there for a moment was to be in the god's presence—or, perhaps, in God's presence. It was an important moment, appealing and moving.

I have often recalled that morning, and reflected on the complex pattern of my experience during those moments. I came as a Christian. I entered one specific, definitely Hindu holy place, with a particular and documented history. I approached one particular divine image, in an evocative atmosphere sanctified by the devotion of believers. I recognized there and then in myself the beginnings of a spiritual experience I would not otherwise have had. I remain a Christian, yet with this memory of a new encounter now "inside" my Christian identity.

II

Reflection on the dialectic of this experience, wherein the non-Christian is truly other and yet truly experienced, constitutes the theme of this essay.[1] That one can approach the non-Christian positively and experientially is not a new theme. Indeed, the widespread acceptance of this possibility is an important and positive development in the life of the Church today. The men and women, particularly in the contemplative orders, who are interested in the experience and implications of prayer across religious boundaries are providing increasingly important and articulate leadership in our efforts to understand the religions around us. In important ways, these pioneers and pilgrims have entered into the spiritual experience of other religions. They have used non-Christian texts in prayers, have frequented and become at home in non-Christian places of worship, have met and prayed with non-Christians. They have inscribed all of this on the Christian map, so to speak, and challenge theologians to think about how to come to terms with these new, boundary experiences.

To a large extent they have also stressed the elements shared by Christianity and the world's religions. Either they have simply highlighted the apparent, shared spiritual and moral values or, more sweepingly, they have claimed that beneath religious differences there lies a common religious experience that is only named differently by different religions, or merely approached from different directions. This emphasis has been a helpful one, a corrective to past attitudes of hostility, condescension or indifference, and to a theological and missionary focus on the world religions as simply a problem to be solved.

I wish to argue, however, that this stress on the discovered common elements linking religions needs to be balanced by a recovery of the true otherness of the non-Christian, as this, too, is experienced in dialogue and study and pilgrimage, and particularly in prayer and worship. When I walked into Tirupati's inner sanctum, I went to a new place, a place particular and local, different and non-Christian—that at the same time was attractive to me. It is the otherness and its attraction that I most remember. I wish to suggest that we need to pay greater attention to the element of otherness of such experiences, and that to ignore or downplay it runs the risk of impeding and constricting the potential vigor and fruitfulness of the encounter with the non-Christian religions. I wish now to describe the risk involved by attention to four facets of it.

First, the risk of an over-emphasis on the shared elements and essential similarity of religions is that it will divert our attention from the situation of pluralism in which we find ourselves today. Whatever we may wish to make of today's situation theologically, and however we may envision the religious destiny of the world, the immediate fact is that Christians live in a world where most people are not Christian, and where most people who are religious experience the divine (or transcendent or sacred. . .) through words and rites and symbols quite different from those of the Christian. Only a few of these people think that their experience is the same as that of the Christian. That there is such a plurality of ideas and symbols and practices, and that the plurality is not likely to disappear soon, is still only dawning on us. It implies a transformation of religious discourse, the contours of which are now only dimly perceived. We must not allow intuitions of universality or indications of the shared elements of experience to obviate or diminish the experience of plurality, before it is fully understood.

Second, the claim that there is an underlying similarity and that we all share the most important elements overlaps with an abstract, intellectualist view of the world which in the long run is ill-suited to the understanding of religions. The "philosopher," if I may use the word loosely, understands the "other" by assigning it a place in her or his already sketched out plan of the universe, usually giving it a hierarchically reduced and off-center slot, which respects its particularity but without allowing it to upset the general plan. The "other" is understood abstractly, as essentially the same as what I already am, and apparent differences are understood to be peripheral and not a necessary topic of reflection. Frequently, this all-encompassing determination of the other is condescending, because it assumes that we have better, more refined categories of understanding than they do, and understand them better than they do themselves, particularly when they insist that their categories, experiences, etc., are really different from ours.[2]

The same reductive attitude is often at work in well-intentioned texts of spirituality and the theology of religions, when these stress the similarities of religions and discount the differences. The religions are just like ours, and are OK. An a priori understanding, implicit or worked out as a theory of religions, is imposed upon the texts and actions and people of another religion, effectively ignoring or underrating or explaining away the important concrete particularities which are the lived material of the religions. At best, a sameness, derived in some way or another and often described in moral terms, is held up as the true meaning of religions. Often, the encounter with the other, in prayer first and then intellectually, is homogenized by an irenic, similarity-seeking rendering of that encounter, which in effect serves only to confirm what we were before the encounter took place. Finally, it is hard to identify precisely the place from which similarities are emphasized and otherness discounted. If one does not rely too heavily on metaphysical and epistemological presuppositions to support an a priori insistence on similarity, one then has to claim somehow to be in the privileged position of viewing religions from above, or outside, or to understand them more deeply than do those who are immersed in their positive particularities.

Third, the stress on similarity makes it difficult to account for, and easy to underestimate, the chances taken by the person encountering another religion. We all know of people, often the young but also older, sometimes unsuspecting beginners but also professional academics immersed in their disciplines, who become very confused, or "lose their faith," after they have seriously encountered another religion. Some boundary is crossed, and the travellers sometimes cannot get back across. In some cases an appeal to psychological reasons is justified—this or that person lacked maturity, looked into other religions for the wrong reasons, etc. But if one stays at this level, implying that there is really nothing to fear in the experience of other religions except in the case where there is some deficiency in the person having the experience, too much that is important is left unexplained. It is more economical and faithful to the data of the intellectual and academic encounter, I suggest, to accept the possibility that what was experienced was itself dislocating, dangerous, that it was an encounter with what has thus far been truly non-Christian and regarding which there are few Christian guidelines, theoretical or spiritual. The non-Christian needs to be understood as something truly different, differently ordered and differently expressed. The experience of it exposes us to the risk of a disorientation vis à vis our Christian starting point, and even to the possible loss of that faith. To suggest otherwise is mistakenly to encourage those who are unprepared for the experience to take ill-considered risks, without the level of maturity and reflectiveness and skill required for an undertaking as momentous as experiencing what is non-Christian. Even if one may hold, as I do, that learning about the non-Christian and assimilating it is most often a positive and confirming experience, it is still necessary to admit that this "other" is by definition something not securely described and already packaged in a predictably Christian fashion.

Fourth, the initial advantages of insisting on the sameness of religions are balanced by the disadvantages that accrue when the appeal to similarity impedes the possibility of something truly new and creative happening in the Christian who engages in the encounter. Initial assurances of similarity may serve later on to defer and dilute "boundary experiences," to silence hitherto unasked questions, to end prematurely the painful process of true growth. Only if we seriously entertain the possibility that there is a different, non-Christian other (or, better, a series of others) can we escape from that closed set of psychological and spiritual mirrors which hem in the person who has already fully understood and explained her or his world.

Without denying similarities which are in fact experienced, and which to some extent make encounter possible in the first place, I wish to argue that in prayer one can experience what is practically, here and now, non-Christian, that which differs from one's Christian experience, which cannot be traced back to the same sources, and which presents itself to us in symbols and actions unlike those which have shaped Christian spirituality. Or, to put it more succinctly: one can meet God in the non-Christian (text, action, person, place) in ways that are not otherwise and presently available to the Christian. This meeting is legitimately attractive and deserves attention, although it opens up at the same time a field of dangers, misunderstanding and even spiritual violence and although it cannot be guaranteed to help every Christian, from the start.

To be more concrete: there are many experiences of the non-Christian one can have, through reading or meditating or travelling or worshipping, that seem at least to draw one toward boundaries where one will have to ask what is possible and permissible for the Christian. I have already alluded to one form of this discovery of boundaries, when recounting my visit to Tirupati. In cases like this, one meets someone else's "scandalous particularity" and, if one takes it seriously, one runs the risk of falling in love with that other. We may find ourselves in the difficult position of loving twice: as a Christian, and as a Christian faced with an other that attracts us. We may have to think through and estimate the depth of each love, and decide what to do. Though foreign travel and a conscious search increase the likelihood of the occurrence of such situations, they also approach us at home, when one meets a Hare Krishna devotee on the street corner and is impressed by his love and joy, when one happens to hear a particularly eloquent and convincing Eastern guru speak on a college campus, or even when one discovers in a non-Christian spiritual text more fruit than one had ever experienced in the Bible. Something new and different works its way into a Christian's experience.

If this encounter with an alternate particularity makes demands of a certain sort on the Christian, there is also another kind of encounter with the non-Christian, by which one is challenged to let go of the "names and forms," the set of particularities that constitute specific paths and how they present themselves to us.

Consider, for example, this passage taken from Paul Brunton's famous account of his travels in India (in the 1930s) and his encounters with Ramana Maharsi, a famous south Indian holy man. Here he describes the effect of his first meeting with the master:

> The minutes creep by with unutterable slowness. First they mount up to a half hour by the hermitage clock which hangs on a wall; this too passes and becomes a whole hour. Yet no one dares to speak. I reach a point of visual concentration where I have forgotten the existence of all save this silent figure on the couch . . . I cannot turn my gaze away from him. Gradually, my ini-

tial bewilderment, my perplexity at being totally ig-
nored, slowly fade away as a strange fascination begins
to grip me more firmly. But it is not till the second hour
of the uncommon scene that I become aware of a silent,
unresisted change which is taking place within my
mind. One by one, the questions which I prepared in
the train with such meticulous accuracy drop away. For
it does not seem to matter whether they are asked or
not . . . I know only that a steady river of quietness
seems to be flowing near me; that a great peace is pene-
trating the inner reaches of my being.[3]

Finally, when asked what he wants to say, Brunton confesses
that he no longer has any questions at all. His busy, inquiring
mind has simply come to rest; there is no need now for a search
and a goal.

The effect of Ramana on Brunton is thus to draw him into the
quietness (though not a total silence) in which Ramana himself had
dwelt for years, weaning him away from his set of controlling
questions about reality. He is gradually led into the most simple
and simply attentive of spiritual postures, in which there is no
longer a need to specify a religious identity for reality.

This tradition reaches back to the Buddha (500 BCE) and before
him to the upanisads, speculative-mystical texts of the late Vedic
period (from before 700 BCE). In modern literature it is still re-
ferred to under various names, such as the "oceanic experience,"
"entrance into mystery," "reaching nirvana," etc. Although this
tradition has clearly recognized that negation itself can become just
one more path, the ancient and modern masters sought to offer the
means for a gradual distancing of oneself from the set of names
and forms with which one is encumbered from birth. Contemporary figures who have come to the West from India, such as J.
Krishnamurti (who died in 1986), question the value of reliance on
specific texts, rites, gods, etc., and urge the listener to let go of
these particulars.

This kind of encounter challenges the Christian to let go of the
various linguistic and conceptual frames by which we frame reality—including our Christian way of framing the spiritual. The ex-

perience of the non-Christian as other occurs in the "letting-go," or at least in the approach to it.

This non-specificity is different from what Christianity presupposes and claims to be, and the difference remains, even if one decides to see the Hindu's letting go as a form of the *via negativa*, and so as proximate to Christianity's own mystical tradition. Ramana, Krishnamurti and others are saying more than that symbols and rites are insufficient or ultimately inadequate; they are raising the question of whether or not the knowing person needs in any way the positive, detailed aspects of his or her received religion, whether a focus on a person such as "Jesus Christ" is really necessary.[4] How far can one go along this path, and remain a Christian? I am not in a position to answer that (legitimate) question here, but only to stress that it is a real question, and that if one takes seriously what this non-Christian path suggests, one draws near to a limit beyond which one could no longer be called a Christian in any meaningful sense. To state precipitously that all religions converge in a highest mystery beyond name and form and that this Indian path is just another, more or less advanced form of what Christian mystics have always said, is to postpone the question of whether something truly different, truly unsettling is meant. It is to lose the opportunity to explore what a Christian might learn from a truly non-Christian deconstruction of religious language.

I have argued thus far that there are good theoretical and practical reasons for seeing the non-Christian as truly other, and that this other can be encountered in prayer. This argument presupposes the possibility of a time-sensitive strategy of deferral, in which one can meaningfully suspend for a time the Christian theological expectation that the world exists only in a fundamentally, thoroughly Christian mode. One must be willing to posit, for the moment at least even if not "essentially," a distinction between what one experiences as a Christian and how one theologically explains the world according to that experience—as imbued with Christ, converging on the truth of the Gospel, implicitly, already Christian, etc. Without denying the latter explanation, and without suggesting that one can retrieve pure, unarticulated experience, one must be able to suspend the formative explanations and instead put a priority on the experience of prayer, remaining for a while attentive to and reflective upon it, without judging it from the start to be a confirmation of what one familiarly, already knows.

To suggest that one can engage in prayer through the non-Christian—a world of experience, including thought, words, symbols and rites, people and places which exist differently from the Christian—is to stress that prayer is an action, an event, and to distinguish it from the theoretical, theological context in which it normally, correctly, takes place. I do not imagine that this distinction can be quickly or easily made, but the effort to achieve it is a necessary component of a true encounter with what is not Christian in its "non-Christianity." Analogous at least is the suspension and openness required generally in prayer: whatever our prior knowledge of God, in prayer we enter the mystery unreservedly and freely without confining it to repeat what we have already çome to expect. While the general openness of prayer cannot entail the expectation that God might suddenly become totally different, it does require a deferral of the confidence that one already knows in essence what God's faithfulness will entail in the future. Likewise, the faithful Christian who encounters the non-Christian needs to be profoundly open to the unexpected nature of that encounter.

If one functions in this open way, one will still, thereafter, return to a Christian specificity. After one has engaged in crossing over into non-Christian experience, one consequently can choose again to be Christian, to remain within the particular framework of the Christian and without labelling this particularity the "merely particular." This reaffirmed specification need not differ in its elements from what one began with, one need not expect to find an expanded set of symbols, new scriptures alongside one's Bible, or even new methods of prayer. Rather, one might find, "everything is the same, everything different."

This second choice for the Christian is new in that when one now chooses to be "limited in Christ," the choice is made within a varied, pluralistic context which includes, for the present at least, other particularities and other choices which are no longer entirely foreign or implausible. In a sense, by the choice to remain Christian one sacramentally restricts and marks that larger world with the sign of Christ, giving it a new, particular order in Christ. This chosen restriction is done by one who, by encountering the non-

Christian, has come to know that this choice is not the inevitable result of a single evolutionary process, nor the only choice in a world that is already, in all important ways, Christian, nor the obvious choice because ultimately the depths of religions are every-where the same and there is nothing else to choose.   In other words, to choose to remain a Christian becomes now a true event, a chosen attitude toward a larger field of experiences in which other choices are possible not just for others but for oneself too; the accidental, contingent quality of faith is revealed in enhanced detail.

Some may then wish to go further and take up again the theological project of envisioning how the universe subsists in Christ. We can, and the community must, articulate a theology of the whole in Christ, even when the non-Christian has been encountered, not deprived of its otherness, and is even, in a certain sense, now within the theologian.   One still insists on thinking through the Christian experience in its universal implications, but now in this new milieu.   This subsequent theological recovery will be necessarily more critical of cultural presuppositions, more suspicious of a priori deductions about religions one does not know. It will also be more specific, as it finds that it has to engage in a theological inquiry that does not reduce to sameness the varied, particular forms of the non-Christian.   Theological reflection on the encounters with religions becomes instead a variety of strategies ordered in a rhythm of a series of particular investigations, reflections on them and hypotheses about them, a consequent return to the particular, etc.

Even if what I have been saying is plausible, it is likely that one basic question remains in the mind of the stubborn reader, a question of fact which might be expanded as follows: "Is there, though, really a non-Christian reality?   Is it not merely an abstraction for the believer to talk about an experience of the non-Christian?   Is it possible for the Christian, after all, to imagine even a part of the world, or some experience in the world that is not already rooted in Christ?"   I agree that there is no point to a merely make-believe procedure by which one pretends to be a non-Christian, or pretends not to have an all-encompassing Christian faith.   But I also suggest that we can and must defer the *formalization* of this faith into a series of statements about the world, and we must be able to critique continually the subtle ways in which that formalization, as already made, shapes and distorts our reception of the other in its particularity. Our formalized claim about the universality of the Christian faith must be consciously positioned as a claim made after, and in response to, experience, and not simply assumed as prior to this experience.

"Praying through the non-Christian," then, is a dialectical activity which claims that one who remains a Christian can experience what remains non-Christian, and that this engagement in the non-Christian is a locus of prayer, of an encounter with God that cannot happen elsewhere, within an already established Christian milieu. This venture into the non-Christian is a risky venture, because its creative possibilities are accompanied by the possiblity of disorientation and loss; it is, though, a responsible and important Christian response to the pluralistic situation in which we live our Christian lives today.

III

In the preceding pages I reflected systematically on the rich and never entirely predictable religious experience of the "non-Christian," an area indicated at the beginning of this essay by reference to the temple town of Tirupati. It may be fitting to conclude by a return to that area of experience, and this time in a way that invites the reader's own response and personal appropriation. I therefore, offer, side by side and without further comment, two small masterpieces of religious literature which have often made themselves heard to me in the midst of my own efforts to understand my experience:

Thou has made me known to friends whom I knew not. Thou has given me seats in homes not my own. Thou hast brought the distant near and made a brother of the stranger.

I am uneasy at heart when I have to leave my accustomed shelter; I forget that there abides the old in the new, and that there also thou abidest.

Through birth and death, in this world or in others, wherever thou leadest me it is thou, the same, the one companion of my endless life who ever linkest my heart with bonds of joy to the unfamiliar.

When one knows thee, then alien there is none, then no door is shut. Oh, grant me my prayer that I may never lose the bliss of the touch of the one in the play of the many.

—*Rabindranath Tagore*

As kingfishers catch fire,
    dragonflies draw flame;
As tumbled over rim in roundy
    wells
Stones ring; like each tucked
    string tells, each hung bell's
Bow swung finds tongue to
    fling out broad its name;
Each mortal thing does one
    thing and the same;
Deals out that being indoors
    each one dwells;
Selves—goes itself; *myself* it
    speaks and spells,
Crying *what I do is me: for that
    I came.*

I say more: the just man
    justices;
Keeps grace: that keeps all his
    goings graces;
Acts in God's eye what in God's
    eye he is—
Christ—for Christ plays in ten
    thousand places,
Lovely in limbs, and lovely in
    eyes not his
To the Father through the
    features of men's faces.

—*Gerard Manley Hopkins*

Notes

Chapter 1

1. Quoted by Nicholas Lash in his splendid book, *Easter in Ordinary* (London: SCM Press, 1988), 25.

2. Cf. John Chapman, *The Spiritual Letters of Dom John Chapman, O.S.B.* Ed. Roger Hudleston. 2nd. ed., enl. London: Sheed & Ward, 1935. This is still the most honest spiritual book I know.

3. Stephen W. Hawking, *A Brief History of Time: From the Big Bang to Black Holes.* New York: Bantam Books, 1988.

4. Herbert McCabe, *God Matters.* London: Chapman, 1987.

5. C.S. Lewis, *The Pilgrim's Progress: An Allegorical Apology for Christianity, Reason and Romanticism.* New York: Sheed & Ward, 1944, 7-10.

Chapter 2

1. Letter of Ignatius to Father Manuel Godinho, Jan. 31, 1552, in *Letters of St. Ignatius of Loyola,* selected and ed. William J. Young (Chicago: Loyola University Press, 1959), 255.

2. Louis Gonçalves da Càmara, *Mémorial 1955,* traduit et présenté par Roger Tandonnet, S.J. (Paris: Desclée de Brower, 1965), no. 256, pp. 188-189.

3. *Ibid.,* no. 195, p. 157.

4. *Ibid.,* no. 256, p. 189.

5. *Letters, op. cit.,* pp. 179-182.

6. Letters of Ignatius to Fr. Anthony Brandao, June 1, 1551, in *Letters, op. cit.,* 240-241.

7. Letter of Ignatius to the Fathers and Brothers at Coimbra, May 7, 1547, in *Letters, op. cit.,* 129.

8. Cf. Thérèse of Lisieux, *Story of a Soul: The Autobiography of St. Thérèse of Lisieux,* trans. John Clark, O.C.D. (Washington, D.C.: Institute of Carmelite Studies, 1976), 192 f.

9. William R. Callahan, "Noisy Contemplation," in *The Wind Is Rising: Prayer for Active People,* ed. William Callahan, S.J. and Francine Cardman (Mt. Rainier, MD: Quixote Center, 1978) 34.-37.

10. Cf. Karl Rahner, "Experiencing the Spirit," in *The Practice of Faith,* (New York: Crossroad, 1983), 81-84 and Harvey D. Egan, "The Mysticism of Daily Life," *Studies in Formative Spirituality,* X/1 1989, 7-26.

Chapter 3

1. A.M. McGrath, *Women and the Church.* New York: Image Books, 1976, 91.

2. Mary Jo Weaver, *New Catholic Women: A Contemporary Challenge to Traditional Authority.* San Francisco: Harper & Row, 1985, 181.

3. Harvey Cox, *Turning East.* New York: Simon & Schuster, 1977, 99.

4. David Tracy, "Christian Faith and Radical Equality," *Theology Today,* 34 (January, 1978), 372.

5. Consuela de Prado, "I Experience God Differently: A Woman's Spirituality," *Andean Focus,* 111: 6 (Dec. 1987) 7-8.

6. Elizabeth A. Clark, *Ascetic Piety and Women's Faith.* Lewiston, NY: Edwin Mellen Press, 1986, 26-27.

7. Anne E. Carr, *Transforming Grace: Christian Tradition and Women's Experience.* San Francisco: Harper & Row, 1988, 8-9.

8. Candido de Dalmases, *Ignatius of Loyola: Founder of the Jesuits.* St. Louis: Institute of Jesuit Sources, 1985, 33.

9. Thomas H. Clancy, *The Conversational Word of God.* St. Louis: Institute of Jesuit Sources, 1978, 22-23.

10. George E. Ganss, "The Authentic Spiritual Exercises of St. Ignatius: Some Facts of History and Terminology Basic to Their Functional Efficacy Today," *Studies in the Spirituality of Jesuits.* St. Louis: Institute of Jesuit Sources, 1969, 2-3.

11. Margaret Baker, "My Experience of a Directed Retreat," in *Notes on the Spiritual Exercises of St. Ignatius of Loyola.* Ed. David Fleming. St. Louis: Review for Religious, 1983, 156.

12. Candido de Dalmases, *op. cit.,* 56.

13. Hugo Rahner, *St. Ignatius Loyola: Letters to Women.* New York: Herder & Herder, 1960, 331.

14. Mary Sullivan and Dot Horstman, "The Nineteenth Annotation Retreat: The Retreat of the Future," in *Notes on the Spiritual Exercises of St. Ignatius of Loyola.* Ed. David Fleming. St. Louis: Review for Religious, 1985, 302-310.

15. Oscar Romero, "Reflections on the Spiritual Exercises," *The Way Supplement,* 55 (Spring, 1986), 102-103.

Chapter 4

1. *The Autobiography of St. Ignatius of Loyola.* Tr. Joseph F O'Callaghan. Ed. John C. Olin. New York: Harper & Row, 1974, 23-24.

2. *Ibid.,* 30-31.

3. For a discussion of the discernment of spirits cf. William A. Barry and William J. Connolly, *The Practice of Spiritual Direction,* San Francisco: Harper & Row (Seabury), 1982, chapter 7.

Chapter 5

1. James Fowler, *Stages of Faith: The Psychology of Human Development and the Quest for Meaning.* San Francisco: Harper & Row, 1981.

2. Northrop Frye, *Anatomy of Criticism: Four Essays.* Princeton, NJ: Princeton University Press, 1957.

3. *Ibid.,* 193.

4. Erik Erikson, *Childhood and Society.* New York: Norton, 1950. 2nd ed., 1963, 258-261.

5. Frye, *op. cit.,* 207.

6. For this discussion of adolescence cf. Lawrence Kohlberg and Carol Gilligan, "The Adolescent as a Philosopher: the Discovery of the Self in a Post-conventional World," *Daedalus,* 100 (1971), 1051-1086; John M. Broughton, "Development of Concepts of Self, Mind, Reality, and Knowledge," in *Social Cognition,* ed. William Damon, San Francisco: Jossey-Bass, 1978, 75-100; John M. Broughton, "The Divided Self in Adolescence," *Human Development* 24 (1981), 13-32; and Michael J. Chandler,

"Relativism and the problem of Epistemological Loneliness," *Human Development* 18 (1975), 171-180.

7. David Elkind, *Children and Adolescents: Interpretive Essays on Jean Piaget.* 3rd ed. New York: Oxford, 1981, 90- 95.

8. John C. Haughey, *The Conspiracy of God: The Holy Spirit in Men.* Garden City, NY: Doubleday, 1973.

9. Albert Cook, *The Dark Voyage and the Golden Mean: A Philosophy of Comedy.* New York: Norton, 1966, 174.

10. *Ibid.,* 177.

11. D.W. Winnicott, *Playing and Reality.* New York: Basic, 1971, 1-14, 38-52.

12. Erik Erikson, *Toys and Reasons: Stages in the Ritualization of Experience.* New York: Norton, 1977, 44- 45.

13. T.S. Eliot, *The Use of Poetry and the Use of Criticism.* Cambridge, MA: Harvard, 1933, 148.

14. W.B. Yeats, *The Letters of W. B. Yeats.* Ed. Allan Wade. London: Rupert Hart-Davis, 1954, 922.

15. Erik Erikson, *Adulthood.* New York: Norton, 1978, 26-27.

Chapter 6

1. Cf. Ana-Maria Rizzuto, *Birth of the Living God: A Psychoanalytic Study.* Chicago: University of Chicago Press, 1979.

2. Cited in Margaret Gorman, *Psychology and Religion,* Mahwah, NJ: Paulist, 1985, 121.

3. E. Shafranske, "Interview With Ana-Maria Rizzuto," *Psychologists Interested in Religious Issues Newsletter,* vol. 14, 2 (1989), 2.

4. Reported in L. Sperry, "From Teddy Bear to God Image," *Psychologists Interested in Religious Issues Newsletter,* vol. 14, 2 (1989), 5.

5. Robert Kegan, *The Evolving Self.* Cambridge, MA: Harvard University Press, 1982.

6. Karl Rahner, "The Experience of Grace," in G. McCool, Ed. *A Rahner Reader.* New York: Seabury, 1978, 197- 198.

Chapter 7

1. Frederich Heiler, *Prayer: A Study in the History and Psychology of Prayer.* New York and London: Oxford University Press, 1932, xv.

2. Etty Hillesum, *An Interrupted Life: The Diaries of Etty Hillesum 1941-1943.* Tr. Arnold Permans. New York: Pantheon Books, 1983.

3. Andre Louf, *Teach Us to Pray: Learning a Little about God.* New York: Paulist, 1974, 13.

4. For further background see Stephen Mitchell, *Relational Concepts in Psycholanalysis* (Cambridge: Harvard University Press, 1988) and J. Greenberg and S. Mitchell, *Object Relations in Psychoanalytic Theory* (Cambridge: Harvard University Press, 1983).

5. Andras Angyal, *Neurosis and Treatment.* New York: Wiley, 1965, 18.

6. D.W. Winnicott, *Playing and Reality.* Middlesex, England: Penguin, 1971.

7. Hillesum, *op. cit.,* 31.

8. *Ibid.,* 49.

9. *Ibid.,* 12.

10. *Ibid.,* 45.

11. *Ibid.*, 1.

12. *Ibid.*, 4.

13. *Ibid.*, 11.

14. *Ibid.*, 12.

15. *Ibid.*, 6.

16. *Ibid.*, 6.

17. *Ibid.*, 6.

18. *Ibid.*, 62.

19. *Ibid.*, 62.

20. *Ibid.*, 36.

21. Cited in André Louf, *op. cit.* 22.

22. Hillesum, *op. cit.*, 66.

23. *Ibid.*, 123.

24. *Ibid.*, 33.

25. *Ibid.*, 130.

26. *Ibid.*, 146.

27. *Ibid.*, 169.

28. *Ibid.*, 169.

29. *Ibid.*, 151.

30. Etty Hillesum, *Letters From Westerbork: The Correspondence of Etty Hillesum.* Tr. Arnold Pomerans. London: Grafton Books, 1988, 146.

Chapter 8

1. Stephen W. Hawking, *A Brief History of Time: From the Big Bang to the Black Holes.* Bantam Books, New York, 1988, p. 55.

2. Edward Teller, *Nature,* 1976, V. 260, p. 657.

3. K.C. Cole, *Sympathetic Vibrations: Reflections on Physics as a Way of Life.* Bantam Books, New York, 1985, p. 46.

4. Peter Kreeft, *Heaven, the Heart's Deepest Longing.* Ignatius Press, San Francisco, 1989, p. 35.

5. K.C. Cole, *Sympathetic Vibrations: Reflections on Physics as a Way of Life.* Bantam Books, New York, 1985, p. 264.

6. R.T. Sanderson, *Simple Inorganic Substances: A New Approach.* Krieger Publishing Co., Malabar, FL, 1989, p. xxiii.

7. John 15:6.

8. John 1:31.

9. 1 Corinthians 13:12.

10. Thomas Merton, The Tears of the Blind Lions, New Directions, New York, 1949, p. 8.

11. Romans 1:20.

12. A. Schmemann, *For the Life of the World: Sacraments and Orthodoxy.* St. Vladimir's Seminary Press, Crestwood, NJ, 1973, p. 19.

13. M. Quoist, *Prayers*, (trans. Agnes M. Forsyth and Anne Marie de Commaille). Sheed and Ward, New York, 1963, p. 17.

14. Lewis Thomas, "The Uncertainty of Science," Delivered at the Phi Beta Kappa Exercises, Harvard University, June 2, 1980.

15. L. Wolpert and Alison Richards, *A Passion for Science*. Oxford University Press, Oxford, 1988, p. 43.

16. Acts 17:32-38.

17. Ephesians 3:20.

Chapter 9

1. Anthony C. Meisel and M.L. delMastro, (translators), *The Rule of St. Benedict*, (New York: Doubleday Image, 1975), p. 86. This is from Chapter 48.

2. The story may be found in Raymond Carver, *Cathedral*, (New York: Vintage, 1984), 59-89. I will cite hereafter as ASGT with pagination from this volume.

3. ASGT, 59-60.

4. ASGT, 87.

5. *Ibid.*, 87-88.

6. *Ibid.*, 88.

7. *Ibid.*, 88-89.

8. *Ibid.*, 89.

9. *Ibid.*, 62.

10. *Ibid.*, 80.

11. *Ibid.*, 82.

12. Simone Weil, *The Need for Roots*. Tr. Arthur Wills. New York: Putnam, 1952, 301.

13. Cf. E.F. Schumacher, *Small Is Beautiful* and *Good Work*.

14. Sidney Callahan has recently written a helpful reinterpretation of the spiritual works of mercy for a "psychological age." Cf. *With All Our Heart and Mind*. New York: Crossroad, 1988.

Chapter 10

1. Throughout I use examples from the Indian tradition because I am familiar with it. Of course, examples from other traditions would also be appropriate, although whatever example is introduced would carry its own nuances.

2. This intellectualistic view of the world is often termed "orientalism" when examined in regard to the reception of other cultures. See Edward Said, *Orientalism*. New York: Pantheon, 1978.

3. As excerpted from Brunton's *A Search in Secret India*, (London: Rider and Company, 1934), and digested in *The Maharshi and His Message*. Tiruvannamalai, India: Sri Ramanasramam, 1981, 11-13.

4. I have represented here what is, I think, the general and radical trajectory of this Indian tradition. However, such sages have always been sensitive to the needs and capacities of the individuals coming to them, and would not be likely to state casually or globally that positive religion is unnecessary. So too, the way in which a teacher's message is passed down often approximates the development of a positive religion.

Contributors

Joseph A. Appleyard, S.J. graduated from Boston College and entered the Society of Jesus in 1953. His doctorate in English is from Harvard University. He has taught English at Boston College since 1967, and is currently director of the undergraduate Honors Program in the College of Arts and Sciences there. He is the author of *Becoming a Reader: The Experience of Fiction from Childhood to Adulthood* published by the Cambridge University Press.

William A. Barry, S.J., former rector of the Jesuit Community at Boston College and presently provincial of the New England province of the Society of Jesus, received his Ph.D. in clinical psychology from The University of Michigan. He taught pastoral counseling and spiritual direction at Weston School of Theology and cofounded the Center for Religious Development, both in Cambridge, MA. He is coauthor of *The Practice of Spiritual Direction* and author of *God and You*, *"Seek My Face," Paying Attention to God*, *"Now Choose Life,"* and *Finding God in All Things*.

Francis X. Clooney, S.J. received his Ph.D. from the University of Chicago in South Asian Languages and Civilization. He is an associate professor in the theology department at Boston College. He has lived and worked for about three and one-half years in Nepal and India and is interested in the spiritual, theological and educational implications of the encounter of religions in today's world. His book, *Thinking Ritually*, was published in 1990 by the University of Vienna.

Harvey D. Egan, S.J. received his doctorate of Theology under the direction of Karl Rahner from Westfälische Wilhelms-Universität, Germany. He was Assistant Professor at Santa Clara University and later at the same university Bannan Distinguished Professor of Religious Studies. He has been professor of systematic and mystical theology at Boston College since 1975. He is author of *The Spiritual Exercises and the Ignatian Mystical Horizon*, *What Are They Saying About Mysticism?*, *Christian Mysticism: The Future of a Tradition*, *Ignatius Loyola the Mystic* and *Christian Mysticism: An An-*

thology. He has also edited and translated Karl Rahner's many interviews.

Mary Garvin, S.N.J.M. is a member of the Sisters of the Holy Names of Jesus and Mary, the Washington (State) Province. She has a doctorate in theology from Andover Newton Theological Seminary. Presently she is on the theology faculty at Gonzaga University, Spokane. She has been formation director for her community and has given numerous workshops in areas of Ignatian spirituality and women in the United States, Canada, Peru, Israel and New Zealand.

Margaret Gorman, R.S.C.J., a Religious of the Sacred Heart, received her Ph.D. in educational psychology from Catholic University of America and is adjunct professor of theology and psychology at Boston College. She is also a psychological consultant to the United States Air Force at Maxwell Air Force Base in Montgomery, AL and to the United States Army in various regions in this country. She has written many articles on faith and moral development and is editor of *Psychology and Religion*, a book of readings.

Richard Carroll Keeley directs the PULSE Program at Boston College which allows students to combine the study of philosophy and theology with social service and social advocacy work. He is the author of an audio cassette series, "The Spirituality of Work," published by Credence Cassettes, and of several articles on the urban theorist Jane Jacobs.

John McDargh received his Ph.D. from Harvard University in Religion and Social Sciences. He is an associate professor in the theology department at Boston College and is author of *Psychoanalytic Object Relations Theory and the Study of Religion: On Faith and the Imaging of God* published by University Press of America.

Sebastian Moore, O.S.B. is a monk of Downside Abbey (England) who studied English at Cambridge University under F.R. Leavis and theology at the international Bendictine Colegio Sant' Anselmo in Rome. He teaches in the theology department and is a member of the University chaplaincy at Boston College. He has published *The Crucified Jesus Is No Stranger, The Fire and the Rose Are One, The Inner Loneliness, Let This Mind Be In You* and *Jesus the Liberator of Desire*.

Dennis J. Sardella is Professor of Chemistry and Director of the newly established Presidential Scholars Program at Boston College, where he has been a member of the faculty since 1967. An alumnus of Boston College who subsequently earned his Ph.D. in organic chemistry from Illinois Institute of Technology, he has published some forty scientific papers on subjects ranging from chemical carcinogenesis to the application of nuclear magnetic resonance spectroscopy to the determination of molecular structure. He has also been an active member of his parish community in a variety of ways, most recently as a leader of the parish RCIA program. Most importantly, he has been blessed with a wife and four children, who serve as a continuing source of strength, joy and sustenance.